The NVTC Executive's Legal Deskbook

The NVTC Executive's Legal Deskbook

Manik K. Rath
Editor

Northern Virginia Technology Council

To order additional copies of this book, contact:
Xlibris Corporation
1-888-795-4274
www.Xlibris.com
Orders@Xlibris.com
95774

Contents

SECTION IV: MERGERS AND ACQUISITIONS

SECTION V: DECIDING WHETHER TO GO PUBLIC

SECTION VI: GOVERNMENT CONTRACTS

SECTION VII: EMPLOYMENT LAW ISSUES

SECTION VIII: ACCOUNTING AND TAX TIPS

SECTION IX: EXPORT CONTROLS AND NON-DISCLOSURE AGREEMENTS

SECTION X: RISK INSURANCE AND EMPLOYEE BENEFITS

SECTION XI: CORPORATE GOVERNANCE

About This Deskbook

The purpose of this book is to create a practical desk reference guide for business executives and in-house lawyers on various issues that inevitably arise in a corporate setting. This book is not a do-it-yourself guide and is not a substitute for legal counsel, but rather is meant to supplement such legal advice. The chapters in this book provide a practical introduction to various legal topics.

I, along with NVTC, thank our chapter authors for their time and expertise. Special thanks to the members of the NVTC General Counsel Steering Committee, and to NVTC, and specifically its CEO and President Bobbie Kilberg, for continuing support.

I am also grateful to LMI for its significant support in the publishing phase of this effort.

Because of the rapidly changing nature of the law, information contained in this book may become outdated.

Manik K. Rath

About the Editor

Manik K. Rath, editor of this book as well as co-author of Sections V and IX, is the Senior Vice President, General Counsel, and Corporate Secretary of LMI. LMI, headquartered in Tysons Corner, VA, is a federal government consulting company dedicated to providing practical solutions to complex problems. Mr. Rath has advised numerous companies on corporate growth strategy, mergers and acquisitions, corporate governance, and labor and employment law. He speaks and writes frequently on M&A and corporate law.

Contributors

Paul M. Bailey, Argy, Wiltse & Robinson, P.C. Paul is a Business Consulting Partner at Argy, Wiltse & Robinson, P.C. He has over 20 years of experience in federal contracting, having worked in both industry and public accounting. Argy provides specialized tax, accounting, and business consulting services. With over 230 employees and three offices, the firm serves a broad base of clients, including the government contracting, technology, nonprofit, real estate, professional services, and hospitality sectors.

Sanjay Narain Beri, Womble Carlyle Sandridge & Rice. Sanjay is a Member in the Tysons Corner, VA, office of Womble Carlyle Sandridge & Rice, PLLC, practicing technology contracts law. Sanjay regularly advises technology companies on the structuring, negotiation, and preparation of their licensing and distribution contracts and the commercialization of their intellectual property assets.

Charlie Bonuccelli, Argy, Wiltse & Robinson, P.C. Charlie is a Business Consulting Principal at Argy, Wiltse & Robinson, P.C. He has over 25 years of experience in federal contracting, having worked in industry, public accounting, and the federal government. Argy provides specialized tax, accounting, and business consulting services. With over 230 employees and three offices, the firm serves a broad base of clients, including the government contracting, technology, nonprofit, real estate, professional services, and hospitality sectors.

Kevin Boyle, Vangent, Inc. Kevin is the Senior Vice President, General Counsel, and Secretary of Vangent, Inc., a leading global provider of information management and strategic business process outsourcing solutions. Kevin has extensive experience providing practical legal and business guidance to high-growth public and private companies, especially major technology service providers to the Federal government. He has particular expertise in the areas of government contracts, corporate compliance, mergers and acquisitions, and conflict resolution.

Michele R. Cappello, NCI Information Systems. Michele joined NCI Information Systems, Inc. in August 1997 and has served as the company's Senior Vice President and General Counsel since February 2009. From August 1997 until February 2009, she served as General Counsel and Vice President of Contracts and Purchasing. Michele has more than 25 years of experience in government contract procurement and is responsible for all legal, contractual, and purchasing matters for the corporation.

David J. Charles, Pillsbury Winthrop Shaw Pittman LLP. David concentrates on general business transactions and mergers and acquisitions. David counsels public and private entities on complex business issues, including the alignment of corporate strategy to accomplish corporate goals. He has substantial experience with buying and selling companies in diverse industries and advising start-up and emerging technology companies. He is currently at Rees Broome, PC.

Brent D'Agostino, AH&T Insurance. Brent joined AH&T in 2000 as an employee benefits specialist. His core expertise includes employee and executive benefit programs, benefit communications, human resource systems, and business process outsourcing for associations and corporations of all sizes. D'Agostino oversees AH&T's employee benefits affinity program with the Northern Virginia Technology Council (NVTC).

Jacqueline R. Depew, Axiom. Jacqueline is an attorney with the Washington office of Axiom, the first viable alternative to traditional outside counsel for complex legal matters. Jacki has 10 years of experience in the areas of civil litigation and labor and employment law with Fulbright & Jaworski and Akin, Gump. She also spent 6 years in-house at Nextel Communications (and later Sprint-Nextel) as Senior Counsel for Employment.

Irma Isabel De Obaldia, Womble Carlyle Sandridge & Rice. Isabel is an Associate in the Tysons Corner, VA, office of the law firm Womble Carlyle Sandridge & Rice, PLLC. Her practice focuses primarily on information technology licensing, specifically monetizing clients' intellectual property assets in the high-tech and software industries, as well as counseling clients regarding the structuring and negotiation of their technology-related deals.

Robin K. Everett, Graduate Management Admission Council. Robin serves as Corporate Counsel at the Graduate Management Admission Council (GMAC), where she negotiates a variety of contracts, including outsourcing, publishing, and software development agreements. Prior to joining GMAC, Robin was a partner in the Intellectual Property Commercialization Group at Hogan & Hartson (now Hogan Lovells), where she focused on outsourcing and complex technology transactions.

Stuart Fox, Argy, Wiltse & Robinson, P.C. Stuart is in the Corporate Tax Group at Argy, Wiltse & Robinson, P.C. Argy provides specialized tax, accounting, and business consulting services. With over 230 employees and three offices, the firm serves a broad base of clients, including the government contracting, technology, nonprofit, real estate, professional services, and hospitality sectors.

Todd W. Harris, Womble Carlyle Sandridge & Rice. Todd is a Member in the Tysons Corner, VA, office of Womble Carlyle Sandridge & Rice, PLLC, where his practice focuses on the commercialization of intellectual property rights in information technologies and digital media. He advises clients on monetizing their proprietary technologies, and structures and negotiates their commercial deals. In addition, Mr. Harris teaches the law of licensing and technology commercialization as an adjunct professor at Georgetown University Law Center.

J. Scott Hommer, III, Venable LLP. Scott is a Partner and Co-Chair of the Government Contractor Service Group of Venable, LLP, a national, multi-service law firm. Scott represents clients who do business with the Federal, state, and local governments and has represented clients on contract administration matters, contract claims and disputes, bid protests, contract terminations, teaming agreements, conflict of interest issues, intellectual property rights issues, government socio-economic programs, and small business matters.

Tamara Jack, LMI. Tamara is the Assistant General Counsel at LMI. LMI, headquartered in Tysons Corner, VA, is a federal government consulting company dedicated to providing practical solutions to complex problems. She advises LMI on government contracts, international trade, and compliance matters.

Karl Knoll, Womble Carlyle Sandridge & Rice. Karl is a Member in the Tysons Corner, VA, office of Womble Carlyle Sandridge & Rice, PLLC. His practice focuses on representing technology-oriented companies and government contractors in connection with mergers and acquisitions, leveraged and management buyouts, venture capital and private equity transactions, spin-offs, recapitalizations, and restructurings, as well as general corporate and securities matters.

Michael E. Larner, Hogan Lovells. Michael is a counsel in the Northern Virginia office of Hogan Lovells. He advises clients on a broad range of commercial and intellectual property transactional matters, including the licensing and commercialization of intellectual property rights. His practice has a particular emphasis on information technology, life sciences, cloud computing, and open source software.

Lance Louderback, Argy, Wiltse & Robinson, P.C. Lance is in the Corporate Tax Group at Argy, Wiltse & Robinson, P.C. Argy provides specialized tax, accounting, and business consulting services. With over 230 employees and three offices, the firm serves a broad base of clients, including the government contracting, technology, nonprofit, real estate, professional services, and hospitality sectors.

Timothy J. Lyden, Hogan Lovells. Timothy is a partner in the Northern Virginia office of Hogan Lovells, where his intellectual property practice focuses largely on trademark and copyright counseling, prosecution, and enforcement activities. He routinely advises a diverse set of clients on various issues from developing and maximizing rights in brands in the United States and abroad, to enforcement of such rights and various intellectual property issues in transactions.

Michael LaCorte, Argy, Wiltse & Robinson, P.C. Michael is a Business Consulting Senior at Argy, Wiltse & Robinson, P.C. Mike has assisted in creating pricing models and policies, calculating cost impacts, assessing CPSR compliance, and helping structure indirect rates. Argy provides specialized tax, accounting, and business consulting services. With over 230 employees and three offices, the firm serves a broad base of clients, including the government contracting, technology, nonprofit, real estate, professional services, and hospitality sectors.

Sajeev Malaveetil, Argy, Wiltse & Robinson, P.C. Sajeev is a Business Consulting Senior Manager at Argy, Wiltse & Robinson, P.C. Sajeev provides a variety of advisory services to corporations regarding government contract accounting, systems, and compliance. Argy provides specialized tax, accounting, and business consulting services. With over 230 employees and three offices, the firm serves a broad base of clients, including the government contracting, technology, nonprofit, real estate, professional services, and hospitality sectors.

James E. Maulfair, AH&T Insurance. James joined AH&T in 2004 to head AH&T's Financial Services department. He has led the growth of the department, which now serves clients of all sizes and currently manages plans with funds in excess of $30 million. Prior to joining AH&T, James worked with for-profit and non-profit clients on both the tax and auditing sides as a Certified Public Accountant with a regional accounting firm.

Philip D. Porter, Hogan Lovells. Philip leads the technology transactions and outsourcing practices in the Northern Virginia office of Hogan Lovells, a law firm with over 2,500 lawyers in the United States, Europe, Asia, Latin America, and the Middle East. He helps clients with domestic and cross-border transactions to commercialize computer hardware, software, data, biotechnology, pharmaceuticals, and medical devices through joint ventures, strategic alliances, assignments, licenses, cloud computing, outsourcing, R&D, and consulting arrangements.

Manik K. Rath, LMI. Manik is the Senior Vice President, General Counsel, and Corporate Secretary of LMI. LMI, headquartered in Tysons Corner, VA, is a federal government consulting company dedicated to providing practical solutions to complex problems. Mr. Rath has advised numerous companies on corporate growth strategy, mergers and acquisitions, corporate governance, and labor and employment law. He speaks and writes frequently on M&A and corporate law.

Ann Robins, Axiom. Ann is an attorney with the Washington office of Axiom, the first viable alternative to traditional outside counsel for complex legal matters. Axiom offers top-quality lawyers at half the rates of traditional firms. Ann has more than 25 years of in-house employment experience. Prior to joining Axiom, Ann served as Vice President of Labor and Employment for Lockheed Martin Corporation.

Joyce M. Robinson, Argy, Wiltse & Robinson, P.C. Joyce is a Founding Tax Partner at Argy, Wiltse & Robinson, P.C. For over 25 years, Joyce has provided compliance work for both public and private companies, as well as partnerships and nonprofits. Argy provides specialized tax, accounting, and business consulting services. With over 230 employees and three offices, the firm serves a broad base of clients, including the government contracting, technology, nonprofit, real estate, professional services, and hospitality sectors.

Dean Rutley, Womble Carlyle Sandridge & Rice. Dean is a Member in the Tysons Corner, VA, office of Womble Carlyle Sandridge & Rice, PLLC. His practice concentrates on emerging growth and mid-market companies (both public and private) with regard to a variety of domestic and international merger and acquisition transactions. Dean also counsels technology clients and venture capital firms in the areas of organization, financing, equity distribution, and venture capital investments.

Christopher R. Ryan, K12 Inc. Christopher currently serves as Deputy General Counsel of K12 Inc. Previously, Mr. Ryan served as General Counsel at Everest Software, as Deputy General Counsel at CareerBuilder, as Assistant General Counsel at Best Software, and as a Branch Chief at the U.S. Securities and Exchange Commission.

David L. Schaefer, AH&T Insurance. David (CPCU, RPLU) is Executive Vice President and a Principal of AH&T Insurance, a top 100 independent insurance broker nationally, headquartered in Northern Virginia for over 88 years.

Curtis L. Schehr, DCS Corporation. Curtis L. Schehr is currently Vice President and General Counsel of DCS Corporation, a professional services company providing advanced technology and management solutions to Government agencies in the national security sector. Curtis has served previously as Senior Vice President and General Counsel of DynCorp International Inc. He also was Senior Vice President and General Counsel of Anteon International Corporation, where he helped guide the company's initial public offering.

Victoria F. Sheckler, Recording Industry Association of America. Victoria serves as Deputy General Counsel to the Recording Industry Association of America (RIAA), whose members create, manufacture, and/or distribute approximately 85 percent of all legitimate recorded music produced and sold in the United States. Prior to RIAA, Vicky was a partner in the Northern Virginia office of Hogan & Hartson (now Hogan Lovells), where she advised clients on intellectual property commercialization matters.

Jon M. Talotta, Hogan Lovells. Jon is a litigation partner in the Northern Virginia office of Hogan Lovells. His practice focuses on complex litigation and counseling clients on a range of commercial matters. Jon is a Co-Chair of the firm's Electronic Information Group, and regularly advises clients on privacy, data security, and electronic information management. He is currently a Council Member of the Virginia Bar Association's Civil Litigation Section.

Catherine L. Thornberry, Carfax, Inc. Catherine is the General Counsel of Carfax, Inc., where her many areas of responsibility include intellectual property, privacy, and employee guidelines and policies. Prior to joining Carfax, Catherine was

Deputy General Counsel of satellite Internet company StarBand Communications. She also was an associate attorney in the intellectual property and technology practices of Hogan & Hartson (now Hogan Lovells) and Pillsbury Madison & Sutro (now Pillsbury Winthrop).

Rick Toering, Womble Carlyle Sandridge & Rice. Rick is a Member in the Tysons Corner, VA, office of Womble Carlyle Sandridge & Rice, PLLC. As part of Womble's Intellectual Property Practice Group and the firm's Electrical/Software Patent Team, Rick counsels clients in patent matters with a focus on the strategic development and procurement of patent portfolios protecting electronic and software-related technology. His practice includes counseling clients regarding validity, infringement, and potential avoidance of third-party patent rights.

Justin J. Wortman, Venable LLP. Justin is an Associate in the Government Contractor Service Group of Venable, LLP, a national, multi-service law firm. Justin's practice involves a variety of procurement issues, including bid protests, compliance matters, prime/subcontractor disputes, and small business issues. Justin also regularly assists the Venable team in successfully litigating bid protests at the Government Accountability Office.

The Northern Virginia Technology Council (NVTC) is the membership and trade association for the technology community in Northern Virginia. As the largest technology council in the nation, NVTC serves about 1,000 companies from all sectors of the technology industry, as well as service providers, universities, foreign embassies, non-profit organizations and governmental agencies. Through its member companies, NVTC represents about 200,000 employees in the region. NVTC is recognized as the nation's leader in providing the region's technology community with networking and educational events, value-added member benefit programs and discounts, a strong and proactive political advocacy presence in Richmond, promotion of state and regional economic development, branding of the region as a major global technology center, and the Equal Footing Foundation, a 501(c)(3) nonprofit charity that serves local area youth.

SECTION I
TECHNOLOGY DEVELOPMENT AND LICENSING

CONTENTS

Chapter 1

The Sphere of Software Law

Todd W. Harris, Womble Carlyle Sandridge & Rice, PLLC

Company executives and in-house counsel in technology-focused companies often handle matters related to the creation, use, or commercialization of technologies which involve interaction among several legal disciplines, including intellectual property law, commercial contract law, and various regulatory regimes. This chapter describes the common sphere of legal issues that executives and in-house counsel of technology companies frequently encounter and is intended to raise the reader's awareness as he or she considers when, and what kind of, specialized legal counsel is required.

Copyright law

Software is subject to protection under U.S. and international copyright laws. Among other things:

- Commercialization of rights in information technology is frequently accomplished by copyright licensing. *Please refer to the chapter "Selected Issues in Business-to-Business Software Licensing."*
- While it is important to understand the rights that copyrights give to a software product's owner, it is just as important to understand what copyright law does NOT protect for licensors or impose upon licensees. For example, copyright law does not prevent reverse engineering, so a licensor must obtain binding contractual promises from licensees if the licensor wishes to prohibit such practices.
- Code developed by independent contractors may or may not be a "work made for hire," implicating copyright ownership. An original work of authorship (e.g., software code) created by an employee within the scope of his or her employment is automatically considered a work made for

hire, which means that the employer is, by law, considered the author and automatically owns the copyright. However, code created by an independent contractor is not considered a work made for hire unless expressly so stated in a written agreement. In the absence of such an agreement, the independent contractor owns the copyright in that work, so the company which hired him or her must either obtain a license to use the work, or it must cause the contractor to transfer or "assign" the copyrights to the company. It is best to be clear in contracts with independent contractors just what is and what isn't considered a work made for hire.

- Databases are not subject to the same level of protection in the United States as in some foreign jurisdictions, and copyright law may not protect a company's interests in its databases.
- Proper use of open source software (for which source code is provided under generally permissive licenses) seldom creates legal concerns for companies. However, some uses of open source software that is licensed on a "viral" or "copyleft" basis may create obligations for the company to disclose the source code of its own proprietary software developments, which would jeopardize trade secret protection for the relevant code. In particular, companies should seek to engage software lawyers who have a deep understanding of the General Public License (GPL) and the Lesser (or Library) General Public License (LGPL), which are the most commonly used "viral" licenses.

Trade secret law

Information is ordinarily subject to legal protections only if (i) it is valuable precisely because it is not known to the public; and (ii) the information's holder exercises reasonable efforts to protect it. The standards by which "reasonable efforts" are judged evolve over time as industry evolves. For a software company, most algorithms and logic employed by its software are embodied in source code, are commonly not patented or even patentable, and are therefore potentially protectable only as trade secrets. Trade secret law is largely a matter of state law, and therefore varies from state-to-state, though most states have enacted the Uniform Trade Secrets Act.

Patent law

The methods that are practiced by software code may be patentable, although applying for patent protection will surrender trade secret protection (i.e., once the application is published by the U.S. Patent and Trademark Office). As of this writing, U.S. patent law regarding software is in substantial flux, and patent counsel experienced in software patent issues should be consulted regarding software patent-related questions. Software methods may not be patentable in foreign jurisdictions, so the protections afforded by trade secrets, which can be maintained worldwide, should be weighed against the value of patent protection in the U.S. alone.

Commercial law—UCITA and UCC

In Virginia and Maryland, software transactions are subject to the Uniform Computer Information Transactions Act (UCITA). UCITA provides legal certainty regarding numerous contracting issues (e.g., the scope of implied warranties), which is usually very pro-business and good for contracting parties. Practitioners should be experts regarding UCITA.

Unfortunately, some provisions of UCITA that relate to consumer-facing transactions have proven very unpopular, and consequently, no other states have enacted UCITA. Outside of Virginia and Maryland, software licensing transactions are commonly treated like sales of goods that are subject to Article 2 of the Uniform Commercial Code (UCC). Article 2 of the UCC was not written with software licensing in mind, so sometimes its provisions can only be applied awkwardly. In states with vibrant software industries, like California and New York, there exists a patchwork of case precedents applying Article 2. However, the law of software licensing remains comparatively more confused (e.g., it is relatively unclear what warranties are implied regarding software when treated as a "good" for purposes of Article 2). All attorneys practicing in the area of software transactions, especially in Virginia, must be well-versed in the interplay between UCITA and Article 2.

Accounting

Accounting considerations, especially revenue recognition objectives, often drive the structure of software-related transactions. Practitioners and executives are advised to consult experienced accountants to confirm that planned deal structures will be treated in the manner that the business intends. Software attorneys must be familiar with current revenue recognition rules, such as the pronouncements of American Institute of CPAs (AICPA) Statement of Position (SOP) No. 97-2.

Bankruptcy

The U.S. Bankruptcy Code, section 365(n), provides rights to licensees of intellectual property rights in the event that the licensor becomes subject to bankruptcy proceedings. Corporate software licensees are often concerned they will be unable to obtain support for the licensed software if the licensor enters bankruptcy, and licensees rely upon source code escrow arrangements, together with section 365(n), to mitigate their support-related concerns. Executives should be aware that escrow arrangements commonly fail to properly understand the requirements of 365(n), and, therefore, escrow arrangements sometimes fail to provide the very protection they are designed to create. Software lawyers engaged by the company should be well-versed in section 365(n) as it relates to source code escrow, and bankruptcy lawyers should be consulted when appropriate.

Antitrust

All intellectual property rights are a kind of monopoly—a set of exclusive rights recognized by law. Though monopolies are generally disfavored by U.S. law (and most countries' laws), they are tolerated on a limited basis in the sphere of intellectual property rights in order to encourage the efforts of artists, authors, and inventors. However, rights holders are prevented by antitrust law from abusing the limited exclusivity that IP law affords. For example, since patents are granted for only a limited period of years, patent owners cannot ordinarily grant a patent license subject to a condition that the licensee pay royalties forever. Antitrust law may also be implicated by the economics of software distribution agreements. Antitrust issues in software licensing are particularly nuanced and are evolving, so executives and in-house attorneys are prudent to consult patent counsel and antitrust specialists when necessary.

Export regulation

Transactions involving software and foreign persons may require engaging attorneys who specialize in export regulation, especially regarding matters subject to the U.S. International Traffic in Arms Regulations (ITAR) or U.S. Export Administration Regulations. Export regulation involving software is more common that one might expect, since the software need not relate to defense or governmental functions, and many commercial software products contain encryption technologies that are subject to export regulation. Further, U.S. regulations define the concept of "export" very broadly, including delivery or disclosure of regulated information to foreign nationals within the United States. Please see Section IX, Chapter 1: Top Things To Know About U.S. Export Controls, for more information.

Privacy and information security

Software owners and corporate software licensees often use software to process data that are subject to various privacy regulations, including the Health Insurance Portability and Accountability Act of 1996, P.L. 104-191 (HIPAA) and the Gramm-Leach Bliley Act of 1999, P.L. 106-102 (GLB). Lawyers engaged by the company should know the basic requirements of these regulations and the basic requirements of information security law whenever they deal with non-public personal information.

Data rights in government contracts

The U.S. government procures goods and services according to the Federal Acquisition Regulation, which includes many provisions related to software development and licensing. Please see Section VI, Chapter 11: Top Things To Know About Intellectual Property Rights in Government Contracts, for more information.

Notes

Chapter 2

Selected Issues in Business-to-Business Software Licensing

Todd W. Harris, Womble Carlyle Sandridge & Rice, PLLC

This chapter addresses selected issues that are important to software licensing transactions between businesses. This discussion does not seek to address consumer-facing transactions, "open source" licensing issues, or general risk allocation provisions such as warranties and indemnities.

Software license grants

A license is a property right, a kind of permission given by the owner of an intellectual property right that authorizes the licensee to exercise the intellectual property right. It is best practice for a software license contract to specify the particular intellectual property rights that a licensee is authorized to exercise.

For example, an owner of a copyright in software holds the exclusive rights to copy, publicly display (or publicly perform), modify, create derivative works, and distribute the software. The owner of a patent that covers a software's method(s) holds the exclusive rights to preclude others from using or "practicing" the patented method(s). The owner of a trade secret, like secret source code, has a legal right to prevent the unauthorized use of the secrets it provides to its business partners.

Commonly, software licenses purport to grant licenses to "use" the licensed software, but those agreements leave open many questions about the scope of rights granted—i.e., whether duplication, public display/performance, modification, creation of derivative works, distribution, disclosure, or use in particular patented methods is intended to be included within the grant. It is better to be more precise when writing license grants, using verbs that identify the particular intellectual property rights which the licensee may and may not exercise.

For example, the license grant might state the following: "Licensor grants to licensee a license to install and use a copy of Software X on 3 personal computers, which license includes the right to make one copy of Software X for each of those computers, plus one copy solely for backup purposes. This license does not include any right to publicly display or perform, modify, create derivative works, or distribute Software X."

License grants may also include numerous modifiers, such as "non-exclusive," "non-transferable" or "worldwide." The variety and implications of those modifiers are beyond the scope of this chapter, but they are central to the licensing enterprise. Please consult counsel as appropriate.

What subject matter is being licensed?

Appropriate attention should be paid to defining the "software" that is subject to the license grant. Does the licensed software include only the compiled, object-code form, or is the source code also included? Is the software merely defined by the product name and version, or are particular file names or functions identified? Often license agreements will state that the software's user manuals or other documentation are part of the defined "software," but this is not always appropriate, since the documentation may be subject to entirely different license grants. It might, for example, be acceptable for the licensee to make copies of the documentation, but not the software, so different grants may need to be written.

Authorized users and affiliates

License contracts should be careful to define the individual persons who may "use" the software. In business-to-business contracts, a corporate licensee consists of the individuals who are its agents acting on its behalf. They *are* the corporate licensee. These persons ordinarily include the licensee's employees, and may include individual consultants and sometimes even business partners. If the licensor does not wish all categories of persons who might be considered the "licensee" to use the software, then the license contract should precisely identify who may and may not exercise the licensed rights.

Common restrictions

Licenses commonly include several restrictions intended to better protect the licensor's interests. A licensor may require the licensee to agree to these terms as a condition to granting the license. Three very common restrictions include the following:

- Reverse engineering: It comes as a surprise to many that it is **not** an infringement of copyrights when a licensee reverse engineers a software product to recreate its source code. In fact, U.S. copyright law expressly permits reverse engineering for limited purposes. However, since the source code of a software product may contain valuable trade secrets, licensors understandably desire to prevent exposure of that source code. To do so, a license contract must require the licensee to promise not to reverse engineer. If the licensee breaches that promise, the licensor may have remedies under the contract and, possibly, under trade secret law.

- Assignment, resale, distribution: License agreements commonly include a prohibition against the licensee's assignment (transfer) of its license agreement, or against its resale of the licensed software or distribution of copies (whether or not the making of those copies was authorized). Copyright law permits someone who purchases a copy of a copyrighted work (e.g., a book) to freely dispose of that particular copy through resale or other form of distribution. This is known as the "first sale doctrine." Therefore, it is ordinarily **not** infringement if a licensee resells its copy of the software, so long as that copy was properly obtained. To prevent unwanted redistribution, a licensor must require the licensee to promise not to redistribute, so that the licensor will have contractual remedies for breaches.

- Service bureau use: A corollary to restrictions against distribution is the common prohibition against using licensed software in a time-sharing arrangement or against acting as a "service bureau" or "application service." All of these terms are meant to prevent a licensee from offering some third-party (aka a potential customer of the licensor) an ability to use the software without having to purchase its own license from the licensor. If every licensee were permitted to resell access to its licensed copy of the software, the licensor's market for new customers could be cannibalized. Intellectual property law does not necessarily prevent a licensee from reselling access to software, so the licensor must procure this promise contractually. This is another reason why it is important for a license contract to spell out precisely *who* may access and use the software.

Software-as-a-service (SaaS)

As software technology and the availability of high-speed broadband connectivity expand, software vendors increasingly market "software-as-a-service," in which software systems hosted by the vendor are accessed remotely—usually via the Web—by the customer's end users. This is broad topic and beyond the scope of this chapter, but it is important to note that "SaaS" is ordinarily just a service, *not* a matter of software licensing. Because licensing relates to the exercise of intellectual property rights, we should ask whether any of the vendor's IP rights are implicated. Does the SaaS customer copy, modify, publicly perform, publicly display, create derivative works, or distribute the software? Does the customer obtain trade secrets? Does a user's act of exchanging input and output data with the remote system via the Web implicate the vendor's patented processes? Frequently the answer to all of these questions is "no," and accordingly there is no need to conceive of the service as a matter for licensing. By contrast, many vendors will grant an ordinary software license to its customer, then additionally provide a service of hosting the software. In that case, the hosting aspect is incidental to the license—i.e., the customer could host the software itself if it chose to do so. Those arrangements are not, technically, SaaS offerings, and in those circumstances most ordinary licensing conventions apply.

UCITA

The Commonwealth of Virginia operates under the Uniform Computer Information Transactions Act (UCITA). UCITA governs software license contracts subject to federal intellectual property laws and has been enacted only in Virginia and Maryland. UCITA is particularly beneficial to businesses because it provides gap-filler rules for software license contracts (e.g., which warranties are implied when a contract is silent about warranties). Companies doing business in Virginia are well-advised to be familiar with UCITA and its unique benefits and pitfalls.

Miscellaneous

The discussion above is a general overview of business-to-business software licensing. License contracts should also give careful consideration to maintenance and support, source code escrow (see Section I, Chapter 5: Selected Issues in Software Source Code Escrow), confidentiality, taxation, revenue recognition, integration and configuration services, allocations of risk (e.g., warranties, disclaimers, indemnities, limitations of liability), economic considerations like royalties, export restrictions, and miscellaneous terms governing interpretation of the contract (e.g., venue for disputes, governing law). Please consult a knowledgeable and experienced attorney regarding your software licensing needs.

Notes

Chapter 3

Considerations in Channel Distribution Agreements

Sanjay Narain Beri, Womble Carlyle Sandridge & Rice, PLLC

Channel distribution agreements represent a range of agreements permitting the manufacturer or licensor of a particular product or offering to market and/or sell that product or offering through one or more partners (i.e., channel or distribution partners). These arrangements can take a variety of forms, but generally describe the rights and obligations of the manufacturer/licensor to provide the product or offering, as well as the rights and limitations on the part of the channel partner to market, and potentially, further develop, package, and distribute such products and offerings to their ultimate end users.

The following are some key considerations when negotiating and establishing reseller, original equipment manufacturer (OEM), and referral arrangements for a manufacturer's/licensor's products or offerings:

- Determining whether the manufacturer/licensor will execute the agreement with the ultimate purchaser or licensee of the product or offering plays a determining factor in the nature and structure of channel agreements.
- Considerations of exclusivity and grants of distribution rights for a particular territory play important roles in managing channel conflict and maximizing the value of the distributed products and offerings.
- When establishing reseller and resale arrangements, significant thought should be given to the allocation of responsibility with respect to support and warranty claims made by the ultimate purchaser or licensee of products or offerings.

- Channel agreements should properly determine the level of control that manufacturers/licensors will maintain over the promises and actions undertaken by channel partners.

Structure of the agreement between the manufacturer/ licensor and the channel partner

Title
Determine whether your channel partner will take title to the products or offerings (including copies of software) for distribution to the ultimate purchaser or licensee of the offering. If so, properly allocate responsibility for order fulfillment and shipment (or copying) obligations between the parties.

Terms for the end user
When establishing the terms for the ultimate purchaser, consider the scope of rights that you will permit your distribution partner to provide to end users. These rights may be subject to your own terms and conditions but consider that ultimately, such end user agreements will need to be affirmed by both your business and the end user. Alternatively, you may want to establish certain minimum terms that your channel partner includes in its agreements with end users.

Enforcement concerns
If distribution partners are responsible for entering the agreements with the ultimate end users, you should determine whether you retain certain enforcement rights in the agreement. Economic incentives may limit the willingness on the part of channel partners to pursue customer violations of their end user terms. Establishing third-party beneficiary rights may mitigate this risk.

Intellectual property ownership
When establishing distribution arrangements, it is not uncommon for channel partners to suggest improvements to a product or offering. In OEM arrangements, the very nature of the arrangement gives rise to the creation of ancillary intellectual property, ownership of which should be properly addressed in the agreement. To the extent ownership of intellectual property in enhancements is granted to a channel partner, you should consider retaining license rights in such enhancements.

Territorial restrictions and channel conflict

To maximize the value provided by channel partners you may want to provide exclusivity in certain territories to particular channel partners. In areas where you choose to grant rights of distribution on a non-exclusive basis, consider establishing an appropriate registration process for prospects to avoid channel conflict and, depending upon payment responsibility, having to provide multiple commission payments with respect to the same end user.

Compliance with laws

When establishing relationships with channel partners, it is important to allocate responsibility with respect to regulatory issues that you may face when distributing your products or offerings. This may include specific provisions regarding complying with appropriate export control laws, obtaining appropriate certifications and registrations, as well as specific compliance with identified statutes and regulations, such as the Foreign Corrupt Practices Act (FCPA).

Termination rights

The ability to terminate the agreement often proves an important issue for channel partners. Having invested in the ability to create and serve a market, the last thing channel partners want to see is to have their rights of distribution terminated. At the same time, manufacturers/licensors do no wish to be saddled with under-performing channel partners particularly if such partners have received exclusivity rights for a particular market. Therefore, it is often advisable to tie termination rights (or termination of exclusivity) to performance obligations on the part of the channel partner when negotiating a channel distribution agreement.

Obligations with respect to the end users

Promises to end users

Channel partners hold responsibility for relationships with end users and therefore run the risk of potentially binding the manufacturer/licensor to terms and conditions established with the end user. In addition, promises made to end users have the potential of affecting perception of the manufacturer's/licensor's brand. To manage this risk, establishing appropriate minimum terms and clearly allocating responsibility to the channel partner are important factors in any channel agreement.

Intellectual property indemnification

Properly scoped agreements should consider the ramifications of intellectual property risks on distribution. Should distribution of a product or offering be enjoined, or subject to a claim of IP infringement or misappropriation, the manufacturer/licensor may wish to control the defense of such a claim, potentially by participating in defending any action by a third party against an end user customer.

Warranty obligations

When drafting channel partner agreements, manufacturers/licensors should determine what role each party expects to play in the event warranty claims are made by the end user of the product or offering. Typically, warranties can either be assignable from the channel partner to the end user (allowing the end user to work through warranty claims with the original manufacturer/licensor) or may be directly addressed between the manufacturer/licensor and its channel partner (in which case the channel partner remains liable to the end user of the product or offering). In all cases, manufacturers/licensors should establish limitations and disclaimers as to the scope of warranties provided to end users.

End user support obligations

Similar to warranty claims, manufacturers/licensors should determine whether the channel partner should have any responsibility for answering inquiries, training end users, and providing trouble-shooting and support. Such support may include distribution of fixes, or even repairs/installation services in the field. Often, channel partners will view these additional services as significant value-added services that they can provide to end user customers. In the event that the manufacturer/ licensor permits channel partners to undertake these services, it is advisable to include strict guidelines, including potential training or certification requirements for the channel partner and its personnel. It is important to consider that problems with channel partner services will often reflect upon manufacturers/licensors.

℘ ℘ ℘

Chapter 4

Top Rules To Follow Regarding Technology Development Agreements

Irma Isabel De Obaldia, Womble Carlyle Sandridge & Rice, PLLC

In this day and age all companies, not just "tech companies," engage in some form of technology development. Whether as the developer or the purchaser of development services, any company that has ever built a website or has turned a business idea into executable software code knows that the negotiation of development services must be taken seriously. This chapter set forth some basic rules that should always be followed when crafting and negotiating development contracts.

Rule #1: Development agreements—you must get one

Every technology attorney has received the proverbial panicked/angry email/ phone call complaining that a business hired a software developer and the relationship soured, and that now (i) the software developer is holding its work product hostage; and/or (ii) the company is refusing to pay. If that doesn't sound bad enough, consider that often no written agreement exists between the parties. We are not talking merely about the young entrepreneur starting a home-based business who hired a fellow garage-dweller developer. These situations arise in complex development projects between Fortune 500 companies which, because they happened to be parties to a prior contract, decide not to consult their legal departments and undertake development without crafting an appropriate new agreement.

Contrary to popular belief about U.S. copyright law, using the phrase "work made for hire" in development contracts does not automatically ensure that the purchaser of services will obtain copyright ownership in the work. Specifically, U.S.

copyright law states that if either (i) the purchaser directly employs the developer, and the development services are within the employee's scope of employment; or (ii) the purchaser commissions work by a non-employee in a written contract, the purchaser is ordinarily deemed to be the author (and copyright owner) unless the parties agree otherwise. However, in the case of non-employee developers, in the absence of an express written agreement, copyright ownership is retained by the developer. Further, if the developer is using its own proprietary code or open source code, or, in the case of websites, the developer registers the domain name directly in its own name, and the written agreement is silent about these "layers" of ownership, the entire ownership of intellectual property rights in the work product may be in question.

In sum, it is critical to get a written agreement in place before starting a project. Often, instead of preparing a separate contract, documenting the deal may take the form of an exhibit or other amendment to an existing technology agreement. Taking the time necessary to negotiate and document the transaction will potentially save you and your company from expending substantially more resources in the event of a subsequent dispute.

Rule #2: Remember that NOT all development agreements are created equal

In the realm of development contracts, it is a fact that one-size does not fit all. A properly drafted development agreement will be a tailored document, not only in terms of intellectual property (IP) ownership but also in terms of the object of the agreement and its business implications.

Consider the difference between developing a website versus pure software development. Both types of development require programming (writing a set of directions to be followed by a computer) and the subsequent testing and re-testing of the resulting computer code. Website development targets various browser platforms; enterprise software is often targeted to one operating system only. Website development may focus more attention to embedded "content," like images or pictures, or to the branding or "look and feel" of the site; enterprise or desktop software development involves more complicated processing algorithms. Particular developers may focus their business more toward website development or more toward pure software. Developers may be individual independent contractors or large outsourced development shops, and they may be located domestically or abroad. All these differences must be taken into account when crafting or reviewing any development contract, because such details impact the allocation of risk between parties, the potential need for cross-licensing, IP ownership, and economic terms.

Whether you are a developer or the purchaser of development services, it is ideal to prepare an optimal form of development contract in advance, and tailor it to specific deals as needed. Ideally, try to use your own template in every deal, particularly if you are interested in keeping IP ownership. Whenever possible, use industry-standard definitions and conventions. The point here is simply that you should *use the right type of agreement for the particular type of development and the particular developer in each case.*

Rule #3: Be unambiguous about who owns what

Development agreements vary widely regarding ownership of intellectual property rights, but here are some of the key themes: (i) *owned work-product*, where the company purchasing services fully owns the development; (ii) *licensed product with a customized component*, where the developer owns the product, but the customer purchases a license to the base product and owns a newly developed component or custom improvement; and (iii) *licensed product only*, where the custom product to be developed will be owned by the developer and licensed to the customer.

Purchasers of development services sometimes feel that they should always own a developer's work product and all intellectual property rights that are embodied in that work product. But this assumption isn't always in the purchaser's best interest, because developers are often able to provide more cost-effective services when they include proprietary code in their deliverables or when they reuse generic materials previously developed on other projects. The interests of both customer and developer can sometimes be protected by proper cross-licensing provisions. For example, if a developer created some truly generic, but useful code last month, it may be able to provide that code to its next customer without having to charge for the time it would otherwise have taken to write the code from scratch. If the developer retains ownership of that code, it can license it to each subsequent customer when needed. Alternatively, if the customer obtains ownership of the generic code, the developer may retain a license that allows it to use and distribute the code in the context of future projects. Either way, both the customer and the developer hold usage rights, and the developer protects its ability to offer competitive pricing.

Always be aware of a developer's use or delivery of technology and/or materials that it has obtained from third parties. Customers surely wish to avoid "re-inventing the wheel," and are frequently happy when the developer can utilize off-the-shelf components at lesser expense. However, even when the developer itself has a license to use particular third-party technology and/or materials, it may or may not have the legal right to deliver the same to the customer. Care should be taken to ensure that appropriate rights are procured for the customer.

In summary, both parties benefit when a development agreement clearly spells out:

1) the pre-existing materials to which developer retains ownership, if any, and what licenses are granted to the customer in these (irrevocable, fully-paid up, rights to create derivative works, rights to distribute, etc);
2) the third-party technology being used or incorporated in the work product, and what additional terms or costs apply;
3) when, if ever, ownership of any custom developments transfers—at the moment of creation, upon acceptance, upon final payment, etc.;
4) when a website is being developed, who registers and owns the domain name; and
5) what aesthetic features, other than mere trademark usage, are required as part of the development effort (i.e., "look and feel," design, images, etc.), and who owns any intellectual property rights therein.

The point here is to *make sure the agreement delineates with specificity what you are getting for the fees to be paid.*

Rule #4: Don't forget about open source

Customers and developers must have a conversation about open source software *before* starting any development project. "Open source" is the generic name given to software for which the source code is freely available or which is licensed to permit modifications and redistribution of its source code, often under licenses that are "viral," requiring that distribution of materials "based on" the open source code must be done, if at all, only in a similar "viral" open source manner. Open source code, precisely for its widespread availability and its low cost (often available without charge), is ubiquitous and is, in some cases, simply the standard.

However, using open source code in commercial developments may poison the venture if done without giving heed to the original license under which the open source code was provided. In fact, some open source licenses altogether prohibit use for commercial purposes. Ideally, any permitted uses of open source components by a developer should be spelled out in the project specifications. Purchases of development services may also desire to receive representations and warranties that no open source components have been included in work product without the purchaser's prior authorization. All too often, the persons drafting development agreements fail to discuss open source-related issues with a project's technical personnel, and unfortunate surprises sometimes occur. Be wary of the use of words like "kernel" or "freely available code," as those may denote that the developer is using open source code.

The point here is that open source components are not necessarily bad, but special care should be taken—at the time the development agreement is drafted—if the customer intends to utilize developers for commercial enterprises.

Rule #5: Compensation drives performance

The common methods of structuring compensation for development services are (i) *fixed price*, where there is a fixed price for the development, or fixed prices for each phase; and (ii) *time and materials*, where payment is based on the actual amount of time spent by the developer on the project and the developer's costs actually incurred for project-related materials. More complex economic scenarios exist, but are not the norm.

Commonly, fixed price agreements are drafted with significant payments up front and final payment upon delivery or acceptance, depending on the agreement. Time and materials arrangements are akin to a consultant's billable-hour style, where the developer invoices the hiring company on a periodic (usually monthly) basis in arrears, and the entire amount of each invoice is due within a certain period after the date of the invoice.

Regardless of the structure, it is in a customer's interest to ensure that at least part of the developer's compensation is contingent upon the work product satisfying specific acceptance criteria.

Rule #6: Be specific about what was ordered (versus what was delivered)

Specifications
Specifications must be clear and detailed. By definition, specifications should not be vague aspirations but thorough technical descriptions reviewed by appropriate personnel from both sides of the deal, and incorporated by reference in the final agreement. Because these documents are often drafted by technical personnel who tend to use shorthand and jargon, there exists some danger that they may not be sufficiently clear to ensure that both parties have the same expectations. If specifications are unclear, then likewise unclear are the duties that the developer must perform and the work product that it must deliver. Clear specifications help to avoid disputes; unclear specifications invite them. Endeavor to make sure that everyone understands the specifications mean the same thing.

Phases
Unless a particular development project is small and straightforward, odds are that it will be structured in phases and the compensation will be segmented and tied to each development phase. The phases are intimately related to test protocols, and the next phase should ordinarily not start until the previous one has been accepted by the customer. As this is also a good way to gauge the quality of the development before getting in too deep, it is best practice for the parties to agree *not to start* unless phases, tests, and acceptance protocols are in place.

Acceptance
Fair and objective acceptance criteria and procedures are pivotal to every development agreement. These should always be tailored to the particular development, but certain principles are universal: silence should not be deemed automatic acceptance; repeating costly tests multiple times may not be to the benefit of either party; and limited periods of time during which acceptance testing occurs should be agreed in advance.

The point here is to make sure the technical draft is understandable. Phased development helps the parties cut losses early, and acceptance should not be a matter of opinion but determined by objective standards.

Rule #7: Allocate your risk—indemnities, warranties, and representations

Usually, *warranties* reflect the relative bargaining position of the parties, but certain warranties are among the most common:

(1) Development should conform to specifications (in the case of software, standards like "material conformity" and "substantial conformity" are common, because no software is perfect);

(2) Services will be performed according to prevailing industry standards;

(3) The developer should not knowingly deliver a product with defects or viruses, and should take reasonable steps to avoid the same;

(4) Open source-related warranties or warranties regarding procurement of all necessary third-party licenses;

(5) Non-infringement of third-party intellectual property rights, particularly copyrights and patents; and

(6) Conformance with all applicable laws.

The usual remedies for breach of warranty are "repair, replace, or refund" subject to a period of time that usually ranges from thirty days to a year. Software, unlike hardware, is a product assumed not to be perfect, and warranties usually cover the appearance of bugs or defects in the code, for a shorter period of time than in tangible products. This is the reason why, ordinarily, a reasonable amount of time should be allotted for the developer to repair, replace, or refund, but the common range of times varies widely. An important provision from the point of view of the developer is the disclaimer of warranties, particularly those implied by law, as implied warranties in the law were not drafted with software in mind and tend to impose standards neither applicable nor achievable.

Indemnity also reflects the relative bargaining power of the parties. Indemnity in the event of IP infringement is fairly standard in development agreements. However, such indemnities can be nuanced, and there may be exceptions (e.g., no indemnity for infringement resulting from the customer's later modification of deliverables), conditions precedent (e.g., offering the developer an opportunity to defend against third-party lawsuits), and various limits on the developer's indemnity obligations (e.g., caps on the amount of indemnity payable)—all of which terms are the usual fodder of negotiation. Risks associated with IP infringement claims are substantial, and the costs of infringement suits may be high, so IP indemnity is often a heavily negotiated contractual term, particularly when patents are involved.

Rule #8: Hope for the best, but prepare for the worst—always prepare an exit strategy

Every contract is analogous to a marital "prenup"—expecting the best from the parties but negotiated while keeping exit strategies in mind. A well-crafted development agreement, like a prenup, should plan for the possibility that the development project might change or terminate. May the customer walk away if it wishes? What are the consequences if a deliverable does not meet the specifications and is not accepted? How will items of value be preserved along the way? What happens to each party's confidential information after the relationship ends? What happens if a party simply decides that its business interests have changed? Provisions that address these questions are all ways to prepare and protect the parties should they find it necessary to pull the plug somewhere down the road.

Chapter 5

Selected Issues in Software Source Code Escrow

Todd W. Harris, Womble Carlyle Sandridge & Rice, PLLC

This chapter identifies several central issues companies should keep in mind regarding the creation of escrow arrangements for software source code. Source code escrow arrangements can be very nuanced, so please consult counsel as appropriate.

For critical applications, software licensees often wish to assure their continued ability to use and maintain licensed software in the event that the licensor cannot or will not provide support. In those cases, licensees often request that the source code of licensed software be made available so that the licensee is able to provide support for itself, including the ability to fix bugs at the source code level.

Most commonly, licensees are concerned that a licensor may enter bankruptcy or wind up business, so that it can no longer provide support. After entering bankruptcy (or winding up), however, the licensor cannot be forced to deliver source code or otherwise provide support, because U.S. bankruptcy law will permit the bankrupt entity to reject future obligations under its existing contacts. To sidestep this concern, licensors and licensees enter arrangements with trusted third-party "escrow agents" who will hold and store the source code for the licensed software until a "release event" occurs. The licensors and licensees may decide what constitutes a "release event," but commonly bankruptcy is included among them.

Following are several centrally important points to note regarding escrow agreements.

Licensor bankruptcy

After a licensor enters bankruptcy, it cannot be forced to grant a license to use the source code. However, U.S. bankruptcy permits a licensee to keep any license it has already obtained as of the time the licensor enters bankruptcy. Accordingly, for escrow to be effective, a license should be granted when the escrow agreement is entered into, even though the licensee has no right to obtain a copy of the source code until a release event occurs.

Source code modification

The license granted with respect to source code should rarely be the same license that has been granted for the object code version of the software. For example, software licenses frequently prohibit making modifications to software, but a licensee may need to modify source code in order to fix bugs. Accordingly, a separate license should be granted that states precisely what the licensee may do with the source code form of the software in the event that a release event occurs.

Deposit obligation

An escrow agreement should specify what the licensor is required to deposit into escrow. If the goal of escrow is to empower a licensee to support itself should the need arise, the licensee will likely need access to more than merely the software source code. The licensee may also need programmers' notes and annotations and other documentation that the licensor's internal developers use. The licensee may also need access to other software tools that the licensor ordinarily uses when supporting the software, such as code compilers. The escrow agreement should carefully define the deposit obligation.

Standard template agreements

Most major escrow providers in the United States have readily available template agreements. These templates will include provisions regarding deposit obligations, release conditions, and the rights of the licensee after a release event occurs.

However, those "standard" terms in the template agreements are not always appropriate for particular licensing transactions, so parties interested in creating an escrow arrangement are well-advised to tailor all of those terms in a manner that makes best sense on a case-by-case basis.

SECTION II
STRATEGIC INVESTMENTS IN EMERGING GROWTH TECHNOLOGY COMPANIES

CONTENTS

Chapter 1

Top Terms To Include in the Term Sheet

Karl Knoll and Dean Rutley, Womble Carlyle Sandridge & Rice, PLLC

Established private and public companies often invest in new emerging growth technology businesses in order to create strategic alliances, create or strengthen potential customers or suppliers, reduce the cost of developing a technology that it will later acquire, or take advantage of the upside potential of related or complementary enterprises that are in the early or growth stages of their development. Strategic investments are typically made through separate subsidiaries having a capital budget dedicated to making such investments or through divisions without a committed capital budget. This chapter summarizes the standard terms that would normally be included in a term sheet by an investor in connection with a strategic or venture capital investment in an emerging technology company (such investment target is referred to as "the company").

Non-binding

Except in rare circumstances, the term sheet should specifically provide that it is not binding upon either party except for provisions related to exclusivity, confidentiality, and expenses (and possibly certain miscellaneous terms such as choice of law, etc).

Investment

The term sheet should specify the total amount the investor will be investing in the company and the percentage of the company's capital stock that it will receive "post-money" for such investment on a fully-diluted basis (i.e., assuming the exercise of all options, warrants, and other convertible securities or rights to purchase securities). The company's value is often also stated pre-investment (i.e., the "pre-money" value).

Type of securities

Most strategic investors and venture capital investors will purchase shares of the preferred stock of the technology company rather than common stock.[1] The preferential return associated with these shares on sale or liquidation is usually for one or more times the amount that was paid for the shares and, to the extent negotiated, any cumulative dividends (see dividend discussion below). The liquidation preferences are generally constructed to fall into one of these three categories in descending order of attractiveness to the investor:

- *Fully participating preferred.* On liquidation, the preferred stock is paid first the amount that the investors paid for the shares or a multiple of this amount (plus any accrued dividends, if applicable) and then participates in any remaining proceeds side-by-side with the common as if such shares had been converted to common.
- *Capped participating preferred.* On liquidation, the preferred stock is paid first the amount that the investors paid for the shares or a multiple of this amount (plus any accrued dividends, if applicable) and then participates in any remaining proceeds with the common as if the shares had been converted, but only up to a certain fixed amount such as two, three or five times the original issue price.
- *Non-participating preferred.* On liquidation, the preferred stock is paid first the amount that the investors paid for the shares or a multiple of this amount (plus any accrued dividends, if applicable) and no more (unless converting to common would yield a better return, in which case the shares have no preference but are instead converted).

Dividends

Cumulative dividends accrue like interest at a specified rate (often 8 percent in venture capital deals) on the original purchase price of the shares (this interest of sorts can also be compounding). Non-cumulative dividends do not accrue, except

---

[1]   Another alternative would be the purchase of a promissory note that would be convertible into equity securities. This alternative may be preferable, particularly if the investment seems particularly risky and the Technology Company would be willing to provide a security interest in the assets that are of interest to the strategic investor.

to the extent that they must be paid as if they had accrued before any dividends can be paid to holders of common stock.

Protective provisions

Most strategic investors and venture capital investors will require that their consent is necessary for the following types of company actions: (i) charter/bylaw amendments, (ii) increase of authorized preferred or common stock, (iii) redemption or recapitalization of stock, (iv) any type of sale of the company or key assets of the company, (v) payment of dividends or other distributions to stockholders, (vi) voluntary liquidation, (vii) change in number of directors on the board, (viii) issuances of securities (with certain exceptions), (ix) taking on debt for borrowed money above a threshold, or (x) any type of interested party transactions.

Investor rights

The term sheet should outline the other rights that investors will receive, which will be contained in the definitive investment documents. Examples of the major rights commonly included are:

- *Conversion rights and anti-dilution protection*—typically the preferred is convertible to common at the election of the holder on a 1:1 basis, which conversion ratio adjusts to allow for each preferred share's conversion into more shares of common to the extent the company makes dilutive issuances that are not permitted pursuant to certain pre-agreed exemptions.
- *Redemption rights*—typically provide that the company will buy back the investors' shares at a specified price (usually greater of the original purchase price and dividends or the fair market value of the shares) upon their request after a specified time period (e.g., the fifth anniversary of the investment).
- *Board representation*—generally at least one seat, but for very large investments relative to combined ownership, joint control with an independent director breaking a tie or possibly even full control.
- *Registration rights*—typical are demand registration rights, either to force the IPO after a certain number of years or which are triggered following an IPO, S-3 registration rights, and "piggy-back" registration rights.
- *Preemptive rights*—sometimes called first refusal rights, which permit the investors to purchase their pro rata portion of any new securities issued by the company.

- *Rights of first refusal (ROFR) on transfers*—usually these rights run in favor of the company and then the investors and are applicable only to transfers by the founders or other large common stockholders, but sometimes these rights are mutual and apply to transfers by investors as well.
- *Co-sale rights*—permits the investors to sell their pro rata portion of shares along with the transferee founder to the extent the rights of first refusal are not exercised, but can be mutually applicable to investor transferees as well.
- *Drag-along rights*—provide that investors, or investors and a majority of the common, can force all stockholders to sell their shares in connection with a sale of the company transaction approved by the requisite percentage of investors/common holders.
- *Covenants and other miscellaneous rights*—additional rights often include rights to financial statements and other information about the company, where board representation is provided, requirements regarding the frequency of board meetings and obtaining directors and officers insurance, etc.

Stock/membership interest purchase agreement

It is not usually necessary to set forth in the term sheet all of the representations and warranties which will be requested of the company in the definitive stock/ membership interest purchase agreement (the "definitive agreement"). It is usually sufficient to provide in the term sheet that the transaction will be "subject to negotiation of a definitive agreement to include customary representations, warranties, covenants, indemnities and other protections." In the actual definitive agreement itself, however, among other things, you would expect the technology company to make representations with regard to (i) its intellectual property (including adequacy of its rights, non-infringement and other appropriate representations to confirm your diligence) and other assets; (ii) its full capitalization, including any options, warrants, or other convertible securities; (iii) its financial statements; (iv) its authority to enter into the transaction and issue the securities; (v) the issuance does not conflict with the law (including securities laws) or its constitutional documents or require governmental or third party consents; (vi) its contracts; (vii) employment matters and employee benefits matters; (viii) full payment of taxes and tax returns; (ix) no litigation; (x) any transactions it has completed with related parties; and (xi) any environmental issues. The definitive agreement will also contain customary conditions to closing, such as the satisfactory completion of legal due diligence, delivery of audited financials, etc.

Founder/key employee agreements

The term sheet should set forth restrictions to be imposed upon the founders and/or key employees, including stock restriction agreements (imposing vesting requirements on some or all of the shares currently held), non-competition agreements, proprietary information and inventions agreements (for all founders and employees that work with the development or handling of intellectual property), and executive employment agreements.

Exclusivity

Typically the term sheet provides that the company will not engage with or provide information to any other venture capital or strategic investor (or related to a sale of the company or other material transaction) for a 30- to 90-day period from the date of the execution of the term sheet. This provides the investor a window to complete legal diligence and negotiate the definitive agreements with some comfort that the transaction will occur.

Conclusion

The above described terms are not intended to be a comprehensive list of the possible terms that can be included in a term sheet related to a venture capital or strategic investment. Each transaction is unique and each term sheet should be prepared with the unique requirements of the transactions in mind. The term sheet, when negotiated and drafted carefully, can set appropriate expectations and considerably reduce the time and costs associated with the negotiation of the definitive agreements.

Notes

Chapter 2

Primary Due Diligence Issues To Consider When Making a Strategic Investment in an Emerging Growth Technology Company

Karl Knoll and Dean Rutley, Womble Carlyle Sandridge & Rice, PLLC

As discussed in the preceding chapter, established private and public companies often invest in new emerging growth technology businesses for a number of strategic reasons. For example, an emerging company may be developing a product in a market that would be a logical extension of the business of a large private or public company or otherwise complementary to its own products or services. While certainly not obligatory, an investment at the early stages of the emerging company's development may ultimately lead to a later acquisition by the established private or public company. This chapter summarizes a few of the primary issues to investigate during the due diligence process when making a strategic investment in an emerging growth technology company.

Purpose of due diligence

"Due diligence" refers to the inquiry and examination of the underlying factual circumstances, contractual obligations, and legal standing of the other party in a transaction (here, the "target). Due diligence is a critical step in any investment or acquisition for a number of reasons, including:

- obtaining a clear understanding of the target's business (and its operations);
- helping in the identification and preparation of (i) a targeted list of representations and warranties to be required of the target for inclusion in the definitive transaction agreement, (ii) a list of any necessary closing

conditions, and (iii) specific indemnification provisions for discovered risks;

- identifying and assessing generally the obligations, risks, and liabilities to be assumed in the transaction; and
- identifying any obstacles to an orderly closing of the transaction, such as voting thresholds, permits or licenses, or third-party consents.

Doing the diligence

In addition to confirming the viability of the technology and performing other business due diligence before investing, consider the following issues.

Intellectual property ownership

One of the most important aspects of investing in an emerging growth technology business (a "technology company") is determining that the technology company has all of the rights to the intellectual property required to operate its business. Some examples of issues you should identify are as follows:

- If the founders of the technology company developed any of the company's intellectual property (IP) before forming the business, make certain that they have assigned all of their rights, title, and interest in the IP to the technology company, and make sure that none of the IP was developed for a previous employer, partner, or someone else who might, as a result, have rights to the IP.
- Make sure that all of the company's employees (from formation to present, including the founders) who are involved with the development or handling of the technology company's IP have signed proprietary information and invention assignment agreements, whereby they agree to assign all of the rights to any IP that they develop to the technology company and they also agree to keep the technology company's information confidential.
- Review each of the company's third-party contracts and make certain that: (i) with regard to inbound IP agreements, any third-party developers of IP have assigned ownership (or sufficient rights of use relative to the business purpose) of the IP to the company, and (ii) with regard to outbound IP agreements, the company has not granted ownership (or exclusive rights of use that are contrary to the business purpose) of the IP to any third party.

- If you think that the company's intellectual property may infringe on the intellectual property of another company, consider performing an in depth review (such as a patent or trademark search) before investing.

Employment arrangements

In reviewing the technology company's arrangements with founders and key employees, you will want to make certain that after your investment their incentives will be aligned with your own. Issues to consider are as follows:

- *Vesting.* If the founders are key contributors to the success of the business, are there sufficient incentives in place for their retention? If the founders' stock is fully vested, consider asking the founders to sign a stock restriction agreement in connection with your investment that would allow the technology company to repurchase all or some portion of their shares (which portion would generally decrease over time) if they leave the company within an agreed period (i.e., replicating the vesting of a stock option).
- *Stock options.* If your investment will significantly dilute the stock ownership of existing management or active founders whose continued participation is key to the future success of the company, will steps need to be taken in order to appropriately reward management's retention and contribution to the company's success post-investment? This might involve increasing the size of the option pool and making new option grants post-investment or implementing a retention bonus agreement or change of control agreement. These measures help to align an active founder's or key management employee's interests with your own in developing the technology and growing the business to the point where it becomes an attractive acquisition target. These programs can also be structured to provide incentives for these key participants to stay on with the company post-acquisition or to otherwise provide desired transition services which will make the company a more valuable acquisition (either for you as the buyer or for another buyer, thereby enhancing your return on investment).
- *Salary/benefits.* You will want to make certain that salary and benefits packages are not too rich (i.e., you do not want to invest in a founder's lifestyle business), as you generally want the rewards to come on exit (in particular if you expect to be the buyer). Also consider receiving blocking rights in the certificate of incorporation or covenants in the investment

NORTHERN VIRGINIA TECHNOLOGY COUNCIL

documents that give you absolute or shared control over changes in compensation after the closing.

- *Severance.* Make sure that the severance package is not too generous and that it will not be paid on a change of control unless the employee/ founder is terminated within a reasonably brief period after the change of control. Failure to do so could significantly damage the value of the company in a sale transaction.

Corporate and securities issues

In reviewing the technology company's corporate and securities records, you will want to make certain the technology company's corporate house is in order. Example issues to consider are as follows:

- *Capitalization.* Review each issuance of securities (including options, warrants, convertible debt, or other convertible securities) made by the company and confirm that the company has taken all corporate action necessary to make such issuance and that such issuance is accurately reflected on the company's stock ledger (or in its operating agreement, if an LLC). Also, review each of the company's contracts, including offer letters to new employees, and confirm that no vendor, customer, new employee, or other third party has been promised equity interests that have not yet been issued. From this exercise, you should be able to confirm that the capitalization table provided by the company matches its stock records.

- *Securities laws/409A compliance.* Make sure that each issuance of securities that the company has made has been pursuant to an exemption from the registration requirements under the Securities Act of 1933, such as Regulation D (for private placements fitting within the specified requirements) or Section 701 (for employees), and that all required filings with the SEC and state securities agencies have been timely made. To the extent that the company has issued options or other equity incentives to employees, directors, contractors or other service providers, confirm that the company complied with the IRS' 409A requirements by undertaking an appropriate valuation of the securities before grant and issuing such securities with an exercise price at or above their fair market value.

℘ ℘ ℘

SECTION III
INTELLECTUAL PROPERTY BASICS, COMPANY WEBSITES, AND INTERNET USAGE

CONTENTS

Chapter 1

Overview of Trade Secrets

Robin K. Everett, GMAC, Philip D. Porter and John M. Talotta, Hogan Lovells

Under Virginia law, a trade secret is information that derives independent economic value on account of being kept secret, so long as the owner of the information uses reasonable efforts to keep it secret. The Virginia Uniform Trade Secrets Act[2] (the "Act") entitles a trade secret owner to a remedy against anyone who "misappropriates" the trade secret, i.e., acquires the trade secret by improper means (such as theft) or uses or discloses a trade secret without permission. Forty-three states, including Maryland, and the District of Columbia have adopted versions of the Act. The remaining six states define and protect trade secrets under common law (state court decisions).

What are some examples of trade secrets?

Customer lists, business leads, manufacturing and business processes, and marketing strategies may be trade secrets, if properly protected. Technology companies often regard schematic diagrams, bills of materials, and computer software source code as trade secrets.

Are trade secrets different from confidential information?

Yes. Information that falls within the Act's definition of "trade secret" is protected by the Act as long as it remains a secret, whereas "confidential information" may be broadly defined as any information that company desires to keep confidential. For example, an employee's personnel file may include information that is treated as

---

[2] Va. Code. Ann. §§ 59.1-336 et seq. (Title 59.1, Ch. 26).

confidential by the company, but because a company does not "derive independent economic value" from it, the information would not be considered a trade secret. Confidential information, which may include trade secrets, can be protected by contract, and the owner of confidential information has remedies for breach of contract if a trade secret or confidential information is improperly used or disclosed. Because both the Act and contracts protect information only as long as reasonable steps are taken to protect it, a company should take the same measures to protect trade secrets and confidential information. The remainder of this overview refers only to "confidential information" as a broader term that includes "trade secrets."

What is the first thing a company should do to protect confidential information?

Identify it. A company cannot protect information it has not identified as confidential, and at the other end of the spectrum, identifying all of a company's information as confidential also compromises the company's ability to protect its confidential information. When some information identified as confidential is obviously public, people who receive company information may be unable to distinguish the confidential information from the public information.

What reasonable efforts should my company use to protect confidential information?

A determination of what efforts are "reasonable" depends on the nature, value, and sensitivity of the confidential information, and different efforts might be reasonable for different types of confidential information that a company has. For example, while a file cabinet in a building with reasonable physical security may be reasonable and sufficient for certain kinds of confidential information like contracts, that file cabinet might not be reasonable or sufficient to protect sensitive information like the recipe for McDonald's secret sauce or the formula for Coca-Cola. Reasonable steps to protect confidential information may include some or all of the following physical measures:

- *Document marking*: Documents, including e-mails, that contain confidential information should be marked. Markings may range from stamping "CONFIDENTIAL INFORMATION" on the first page of a document, or including it in the footer of each page, to a notice like the following:

THIS DOCUMENT CONTAINS INFORMATION THAT IS TREATED
AS CONFIDENTIAL AND PROPRIETARY BY ABC CORPORATION.

- *Document destruction*: Confidential information that a company is not required to retain should be discarded in confidential waste receptacles, and then routinely shredded, and purged from electronic storage.
- *Document numbering and inventory*: A company should maintain control over access to documents containing particularly sensitive information. Sensitive documents may be numbered to facilitate tracking their distribution, conducting inventories of their whereabouts, and identifying in an access log individuals who have had access to the confidential information.
- *Facility security*: Main entrances to company facilities should be monitored to prevent unauthorized entry and should be locked when unattended, and other entrances to the company facilities should be locked at all times. If the size of the company or organization of the workforce precludes mutual familiarity among employees, employees should be required to wear badges identifying themselves as company employees. All visitors should sign in and out, stating the date, reason for their visit, the company employee(s) with whom they are meeting, and arrival and departure times; should wear a badge identifying them as a visitor; and should be accompanied by company personnel at all times during their visit.

Electronic measures

- *Computer security*: Access to a company's computer system should require diligent password use, and disclosure of passwords should be prohibited. Transfers of confidential information to employee home computers should be prohibited or carefully restricted.
- *Portable electronic devices*: Where possible, confidential information should not be stored in laptops, PDAs, flash drives, or similar devices that are susceptible to loss and theft. Access to portable devices that contain confidential information should be limited by passwords and other access authorization technology.
- *E-mail encryption*. Consideration should be given to encrypting e-mails that transmit confidential information outside a company.

Measures with employees

- *Employee confidentiality agreements*: A company should enter into confidentiality agreements, which may be part of broader intellectual property agreements that address inventions and copyrightable works. Although employees have a legal obligation to protect their employer's confidential information, confidentiality agreements serve an educational purpose for employees who may not know the law or recognize the importance of protecting confidential information.
- *Electronic equipment and social media policies.* A company should adopt policies that restrict copying of confidential information and unauthorized disclosure of confidential information in e-mails and social media. Employees should be required to verify that they have read these policies annually, and a company with sensitive information should conduct periodic employee training about the subject matter of the policies.
- *Employee exit interviews.* A company should conduct exit interviews with departing employees to (a) remind them of their confidentiality obligations and the types of confidential information to which they have had access and (b) request return of confidential information in paper and electronic form, computer hardware and software, and information security measures such as keys, badges, and passwords for computers and physical locking mechanisms. A company should also consider asking departing employees to sign a statement acknowledging their continuing obligations to protect the company's confidential information and warranting that they have not retained possession of any such information.

Measures with third parties

- *Third-party confidentiality agreements*: Prior to disclosure of information to a third party, such as a potential customer, supplier, or strategic alliance member, a company should enter into a non-disclosure agreement with the third party.

- *Other contracts*: A company should include a confidentiality provision in all contracts that may involve third-party access to or use of confidential information. A company should also consider whether a contract for development should state that the deliverables developed under the contract are "confidential information" of one of the parties.

Notes

Chapter 2

Why Companies Need Legal Terms Governing Their Websites

Philip D. Porter, Hogan Lovells, Victoria F. Sheckler, RIAA,
and Jon M. Talotta, Hogan Lovells

Websites that are accessible by the general public, from basic informational websites to more sophisticated interactive or commerce driven websites, may expose their operators to unintended risks. Below are some questions a company operating a website should consider to limit some of those risks.[3]

Should a company publish legal terms on its website?

Yes. All websites should publish legal terms that, at a minimum, (a) let visitors know what they may do with content (e.g., text, graphics, photographs, audio, and video) that is published on the website, (b) disclaim warranties for website content, (c) limit the company's liability arising out of or in connection with the website, and (d) identify the jurisdiction whose law governs the interpretation of the legal terms.

---

[3]   Websites that are accessible by the general public may be accessed from anywhere in the world, and individual jurisdictions have very different laws that may be applicable to website operation. A company whose intended website audience includes visitors who are outside the United States should check the laws of other jurisdictions from which the company reasonably expects to draw visitors.

Should a company use any other legal terms if its website includes social media tools?

Yes. Social media tools facilitate the publication of content provided by visitors. Visitors may inadvertently or intentionally upload content to the website that infringes third-party copyrights or trademarks, violates third-party rights of privacy and publicity, discloses confidential information without authorization, is libelous or defamatory, or is otherwise unacceptable to the company.

To protect against copyright infringement claims arising out of content posted by visitors, a company should comply with the requirements of the Digital Millennium Copyright Act and designate an agent with the U.S. Copyright Office to whom third parties who believe that their copyright is infringed by content on the website can send notices. Next, although the Communications Decency Act of 1996 can protect website operators against other types of liability for content posted by visitors, to further protect the company, legal terms for websites that include social media tools should (a) notify visitors that the company does not monitor or accept responsibility for content that visitors post and does not endorse or agree with comments, opinions or statements posted by visitors, (b) reserve for the company the right to reject, refuse to post, or remove any content provided by visitors, and (c) require visitors to represent and warrant that they own or have the legal right to post any content they provide and that the content they provide does not violate any third-party rights.

Are legal terms that are accessed from a link at the foot of a company's home page enforceable?

Often they are. U.S. courts typically enforce legal terms accessed from a link at the foot of a website's home page, often called "browse-wrap terms," if they contain no "surprising" terms. The terms described in response to the first question above are typically regarded as unsurprising and are generally enforceable in the United States. Courts have not always enforced provisions that require arbitration of disputes with the website operator or that require all lawsuits against the operator to be brought in courts in the operator's home state.

Is there a more reliable alternative to browse-wrap terms?

Yes. Legal terms presented with an opportunity to click "I agree," often called "click-wrap terms," are more reliably enforceable because they demonstrate the visitor's affirmative assent to the terms. Click-wrap terms are often used as a condition of admission to a limited-access website or a limited-access area in a publicly accessible website, for legal terms whose validity is very important to a website operator. For example, a company may use a limited access website to make company confidential information available to potential purchasers of the company or to prospective bidders who have received a company-issued RFP, subject to confidentiality obligations.

What form of legal terms should be used for a company website that offers goods, services, or information for sale?

While a browse-wrap license may be sufficient for sale of low-risk merchandise, online merchants offering higher-risk products have a greater interest in reliably enforceable warranty disclaimers, liability limitations, and payment obligations. The Uniform Electronic Transactions Act (UETA), which has been adopted by 47 states (including Virginia and Maryland) and the District of Columbia, states that a contract is not invalid merely because it is in electronic form and further states that it applies to parties who have agreed to conduct transactions by electronic means.

In practice, many online merchants use two stages of click-wrap terms. The first click signifies a purchaser's agreement to applicable online terms and the full price, and a second click signifies the purchaser's understanding and acknowledgment of, and agreement to, the terms of the transaction. The transaction is completed only after the second click.

What must a company do to change the legal terms on its website?

Many websites include a notice in their legal terms to the effect that they may make changes in the legal terms at any time, and that visitors should review the legal terms periodically and will be bound by any changes if they use the website after the changes are published. In early 2009, a court in Texas refused to enforce a new provision that was added to legal terms in accordance with a notice of this type. As yet, no other courts have reached a similar result. A company that wishes to change any of its online legal terms should post a notice of the date of the most recent change to those terms and maintain a record of the various forms of legal terms it has used and the dates when they were in use.

A record of when the website's legal terms first become binding on individual users can be very helpful, but as a practical matter one is rarely available except in connection with online purchases. When enforceability of online legal terms is very important (most often in the case of click-wrap terms), the company should require visitors to click "I agree" to the revised terms before readmission to a limited access website or use of other website functions to which the legal terms apply.

Should a company publish a privacy policy on its web site?

The Children's Online Privacy Protection Act requires websites that collect information from children under the age of 13 to publish privacy policies, and California law requires operators of commercial websites or online services that collect personally identifiable information from users in California to publish privacy policies. Since websites can be accessed from any geographic location, the California statute has potentially wide applicability.

Some service providers require their customers to publish privacy policies. For example, Visa Inc. imposes such a requirement on online merchants that accept Visa card payments. Unless a company is subject to a legal or contractual requirement to publish a privacy policy, doing so is voluntary. However, many website visitors look for a website's privacy policy before providing personal information in connection with their use of a website, and many website operators publish privacy policies.

What should a company's privacy policy contain?

First and foremost, the contents of a company's privacy policy must be accurate. Copying a privacy policy from another website or using a template privacy policy obtained online is a high-risk practice, since the contents of that policy may not accurately describe the company's practices with respect to the collection, retention, use, and disclosure of personal information. Publication of a website privacy policy subjects a company to the jurisdiction of the Federal Trade Commission (FTC), and the FTC regards publication of inaccurate information in a privacy policy as an unfair trade practice. The FTC has promoted the following four fair information practices, which a company should implement when preparing a privacy policy:

- *Notice.* A website privacy policy should describe the types of personal information being gathered, the way it will be used, with whom it will be shared, who is gathering the information, any options the user has regarding its use and disclosure, and security procedures in place to prevent unauthorized access, modification, n or loss.
- *Choice.* A website should offer visitors choices as to how their personally identifiable information is used beyond the use for which the information was provided (for example, to apply for employment, purchase a product, or obtain confidential information).
- *Security.* A website operator should take reasonable and appropriate measures to protect the confidentiality and integrity of personally identifiable information that is collected.
- *Access.* A website operator should provide visitors opportunities to review and contest the accuracy and completeness of personally identifiable information collected about them.

Notes

Chapter 3

Key Components of Policies Used by Companies That Give Their Employees Internet Access

Philip D. Porter and Jon M. Talotta, Hogan Lovells, and
Catherine L. Thornberry, Carfax, Inc.

Companies that give their employees Internet access have a legitimate interest in the working time that their employees spend on the Internet and the activities in which they engage, which can have both legal and commercial implications. Such companies should consider adopting a policy that guides employee use of the Internet and prohibits uses in which the company does not want employees to engage. Before developing an Internet usage policy, a company should evaluate the purposes for which it gives its employees Internet access and create reasonable and realistic guidelines to minimize risk and liability exposure. Further, a company should consider whether it has the resources to monitor and enforce such a policy (as failure to do so can have unintended negative consequences). Acceptance and adoption of an Internet policy can be improved if a company educates its employees as to the risks—to the company and individual employees—inherent in Internet usage not in accordance with the company's policy.

Topics that an Internet usage policy applicable to employees in the United States should address include the following (companies should consult applicable laws in jurisdictions outside the United States where any employees to whom policies will apply are located).

Business and personal use

Companies provide Internet access to increase productivity rather than diminish it.

- While absolute prohibition of employees' use of a company's Internet access for personal purposes is probably unrealistic, many companies' Internet usage policies remind employees that Internet access is provided for business purposes and that use of the Internet for personal reasons should be kept to an absolute minimum and should not interfere with work.
- Internet usage policies frequently prohibit use of company-provided Internet access, including after normal working hours, to support an employee's own business or an employee's work for another employer.
- To avoid consumption of bandwidth and reduction of speed of content access, many Internet usage policies prohibit employees from listening to the radio, watching digital entertainment videos and television programs, and playing online games at all times through company-provided Internet access.
- Internet usage policies typically prohibit employees—or automatically block employees—from using company-provided access from sending, displaying, downloading, printing and or storing images, text, graphics, or other digital files, or accessing FTP or other sites, that contain any of the following:
  ◇ pornographic or sexually explicit material; or
  ◇ material that may be offensive to individuals of a specific race, color, gender, religion, sexual orientation or ethnic or national origin or individuals with a recognizable physical characteristic or disability, or that otherwise could reasonably be expected to be offensive to others.

Many Internet usage policies notify employees that websites they visit using the company's technology, including Internet access from home through the company's network, may record the company's name on the website's visitor log.

Use of social media

Social media websites allow visitors to upload and publish content and opinions, provide commentary and responses to the content and opinions posted by others, and provide information about themselves. Some companies use social media for business purposes (interaction with customers and prospective customers) and allow or encourage their employees to do the same. Given the popularity of social media, prohibiting its use may be unrealistic, and providing guidance for employee use of social media may be much more productive. In addition to general guidelines for employee use of the Internet, which are fully applicable to use of social media, companies should consider providing some or all of the following guidelines that are more specific to social media:

- Most Internet usage policies prohibit posting company confidential information, and company training programs should reinforce the care employees should take when disclosing any company information on the Internet to be sure that proposed postings include no confidential information.

- Internet usage policies often warn employees to be judicious about posting photos or personally identifiable information about themselves online out of concern that such information might result in a loss of business if viewed as inappropriate by prospective customers or business affiliates. Even greater motivation for care in posting information may be fostered by suggesting that employees consider how identity thieves, other criminals, and future employers might use personal information they post.

- Many Internet usage policies prohibit employees from using company-provided Internet access to disseminate jokes, cartoons, and other content that might embarrass the company.

- Internet usage policies should advise employees that references to the company and any of its products and services must be accurate and that the employee's role in the company be transparent and disclosed. References to competitors also must be accurate.

  ◇ Many Internet usage policies instruct employees that only certain authorized employees are permitted to post content that could be attributed to the company, and to participate in chat rooms, post messages to bulletin boards, contribute to listservs, or publish a blog.

  ◇ Internet usage policies may prohibit employees from commenting online about the company or its products, as such postings can give rise to claims of improper endorsement if they cannot be substantiated or if related compensation is not disclosed. The Federal Trade Commission recently revised its advertising guidelines "Guides Concerning the Use of Endorsements and Testimonials in Advertising" to provide guidance on endorsement and testimonial ads. The revised guidelines, which became effective December

1, 2009, may be found in 16 C.F.R. Part 255 (www.ftc.gov/
os/2009/10/091005
◇ revisedendorsementguides.pdf).

Expectation of privacy

An Internet usage policy should remind employees that they have no expectation of privacy in their use of the Internet with company equipment and company-provided Internet access and that the company has the right to monitor Internet usage.

Copyright/trademark

An Internet usage policy should require employees to respect the intellectual property rights of third parties in online content (e.g., text, graphics, names, logos, photographs, audio, and video). The fact that content is posted on the Internet does not mean that it is in the public domain or that it may be freely copied and circulated. Before making or distributing (on paper or electronically) copies of any online content, employees should review and abide by legal terms published on the website where the content is found. Legal terms often provide that content may be used only for personal, noncommercial purposes. Internet usage policies should obligate employees to verify that any content retrieval, downloading, reproduction, distribution, sharing, storage, modification, display and performance in which they engage is permitted by applicable legal terms or that the employee has secured appropriate permission from the copyright owner to make such use of the materials. Internet usage policies often prohibit participation in peer-to-peer file sharing of music, videos, and other copyrightable content.

Third-party software

Internet usage policies often prohibit employees from downloading software onto company systems from the Internet. Such usage not only risks virus infection but also exposes the company to copyright infringement allegations if the company is audited and license documentation for downloaded software is unavailable. Many Internet usage policies reserve the company's right to remove unauthorized computer software without notice, and/or block an employee's ability to download unauthorized software.

৩ ৩ ৩

Chapter 4

Overview of Copyrights

Michael E. Larner, Hogan Lovells, and Christopher R. Ryan, K12 Inc.

Copyright law is a form of intellectual property protection intended to protect the creative endeavors of authors. Copyright is protected by federal law in the United States, pursuant to the Copyright Act of 1976. This chapter summarizes key issues related to U.S. copyright protection.

Scope of copyright protection

Copyright protects original works of authorship that are fixed in a tangible form of expression.

- Examples of works of authorship include text, photographs, audio, video, graphics, and computer programming in source code and object code form.
- Unlike patent protection, copyright affords no protection for ideas, concepts, or inventions. Copyright only protects the expression of the ideas, concepts, and inventions.
- No registration is required with the copyright office to secure a copyright, although registration provides several important advantages (see below). Copyright protection starts automatically at the time of creation, as soon as the work of authorship is fixed in a tangible form of expression.

Exclusive rights of copyright owner

The owner of the copyright has the following exclusive rights, which the owner can exercise or authorize others to exercise:

- right to reproduce the work,

- right to prepare derivative works (i.e., modify the work),
- right to distribute copies of the work,
- right to publicly perform the work, and
- right to publicly display the work.

Copyright infringement occurs when a party exercises one of these exclusive rights without the copyright owner's permission.

Ownership of copyright

Copyright ownership is initially with the author of the work.

In most instances, the author of the work is the party that originally created the work. However, if the work qualifies as a "work made for hire" (see section below), the employer or other party that commissioned the work is considered the author of the work.

Ownership may be assigned to another party, if such assignment is in writing and signed by the party transferring its rights.

Works made for hire

A work of authorship is only a "work made for hire" if it passes one of two tests:

- The work was prepared by an employee within the scope of employment, or
- The work was prepared by a non-employee under a written contract which specifies the work will be a "work made for hire" *and* the work falls within one of nine fairly narrow statutory categories. Therefore, if a company hires an independent contractor to develop a copyrightable work, even if the parties clearly state their intentions in a contract for the work to be considered a "work made for hire," if the work does not fall within one of the nine statutory categories, the independent contractor is the copyright owner.

Length of protection

For works created on or after January 1, 1978, copyright protection generally lasts the length of the author's life plus 70 years. However, there are specific rules for different types of work. For example:

- joint works created by multiple authors are protected until 70 years after the last surviving author's death, and
- works made for hire are protected for 95 years from publication or 120 years from creation, whichever is shorter.

For works created prior to January 1, 1978, the length of protection is subject to more variables, and the applicable statute should be consulted to determine the protection period.

Fair use

The fair use doctrine provides an affirmative defense to a claim of copyright infringement, for purposes such as criticism, parody, reporting, and teaching. Courts consider the following four factors in determining whether an unauthorized use of a copyrighted work qualifies as a fair use:

- purpose and character of the use, including whether such use is of a commercial nature or is for nonprofit educational purposes,
- nature of the work,
- amount and substantiality of the portion used in relation to the copyrighted work as a whole, and
- effect of the use upon the potential market for, or value of, the work.

However, the fair use doctrine is often misinterpreted by some to permit the use of another party's copyrighted work, as long as the user feels it is "fair." One must instead carefully examine the four factors above when evaluating fair use.

Copyright notice

The use of a copyright notice is no longer required under United States copyright law. However, the use of a copyright notice is a recommended best practice. A copyright notice is simple and inexpensive, serves to identify the copyright owner, and informs the public that the work is protected.

Advantages of copyright registration

Although not required for copyright protection, the registration process offered by the U.S. Copyright Office (www.copyright.gov) is inexpensive and relatively easy. Registration with the U.S. Copyright Office also offers the copyright owner several important benefits:

- Registration is required before bringing a federal copyright infringement suit.
- A registration issued within the first 5 years of publication establishes prima facie evidence of the validity of the copyright.
- Registration within 3 months of first publication or prior to infringement can result in an award of statutory damages (i.e., automatic monetary damages), which is helpful because ordinarily the copyright owner would need to prove actual damages and lost profits.

Many of the fundamental rules and issues relating to copyright law are commonly misunderstood, including the scope of copyright protection, the ownership of works made for hire, the fair use doctrine, copyright notice requirements, and the copyright registration process. This chapter is intended to provide a quick reference to address these common misunderstandings and other related issues regarding copyright protection in the United States.

Chapter 5

Overview of Trademarks

Timothy J. Lyden, Hogan Lovells, and Christopher R. Ryan, K12 Inc.

Even though a trademark can be a company's most important asset, trademark law is a form of intellectual property protection intended to protect consumers. A trademark is a word, phrase, design, or some other symbol (such as a color, scent, or sound) that is used to identify the source of products (or both products and services) and to distinguish such products and/or services from those of others. A service mark is a word, phrase, design, or some other symbol that is used to identify the source of services. Trademarks and service marks, often referred to collectively as "trademarks" or "marks," also serve to indicate that all goods bearing a mark and all services in connection with which a mark is used are of a certain quality, good or bad.

In the United States, trademarks are protected by common law as well as federal and state statutes.

Territoriality of trademark rights

Trademark rights are territorial in nature. Absent filings in various jurisdictions around the world, through one or more of various filing options available, it would be impossible to claim trademark rights worldwide.

The United States

In the United States, one acquires trademark rights merely through use of a mark on products and/or in connection with services. Such common law trademark rights provide protection in the geographic area in which a trademark owner uses a mark, plus in some cases, a zone of natural or reasonable expansion.

Outside the United States

In many other countries throughout the world—including Brazil, China, and the United Arab Emirates, for example—a party must obtain a trademark registration to acquire trademark rights and establish priority in relation to third parties.

Trademark registration in the United States

State and federal statutes can expand the scope of rights of a trademark rights holder beyond those available under common law, providing nationwide use and constructive priority in relation to third parties upon issuance of certain federal registrations on the Principal Register. In addition, federal registration with the U.S. Patent and Trademark Office (www.uspto.gov) can provide additional remedies to trademark rights holders under certain circumstances. Similarly, registration of a mark on the state level can provide additional rights and/or remedies under state law. In Virginia, the State Corporation Commission (www.scc.virginia.gov/srf) is the agency that processes applications for registration of marks. (See VA. Code Ann. § 59.1-92.1 et seq.)

Not all marks are created equal

As shown in the table below, there are four categories of marks ranging from the strongest (broadest protection possible to enforce rights against others) to the weakest (no ability to claim exclusive rights):

Type of Mark	Information	Example	Strength
Fanciful	Arbitrary (existing word but no connection to the good or service) or made-up word.	"Apple" for computers	Strongest legal protection.
Suggestive	Suggest a quality or function of the good or service but require some imagination.	"Sudsy" for soap	Fairly strong legal protection.
Descriptive	Highly descriptive of the good or service.	"Pralines 'N Cream" for ice cream	Weak legal protection.
Generic	Common words or phrases for the good or service—already used widely.	"Apple" for fruit from an apple tree	No legal protection.

Assignment of trademark rights

In the United States and many other jurisdictions, trademarks can be assigned only with the goodwill associated with the business to which they relate. An assignment of trademark that does not include the goodwill associated with the business is considered invalid. Note that any trademark license must contain quality control provisions, or the trademark rights holder (licensor) could lose rights in the mark.

Trademark notice

Although not required, a trademark notice is a good idea to place others on notice of one's rights, or claimed rights, in a trademark. The federal registration notice (®) is reserved for trademarks that are registered (not pending) with the U.S. Patent and Trademark Office, and correct use can increase the scope and amount of remedies available in certain infringement actions. Use ® for federally registered marks—when using them in connection with the goods and/or services for which they are registered.

Unregistered trademarks and trademarks that are the subject of pending federal applications for registration (or are registered with state trademark offices) should not be used with the ® symbol. Instead, use either TM to designate trademarks used in connection with goods (or with goods and services) or SM to designate a service mark used only in connection with services.

Also, make it clear who owns the mark by accompanying use of the mark in a brochure or in advertising literature with a notation of ownership in one of the following forms:

- The mark Coke® is a federally registered trademark of The Coca-Cola Company.
- The NVTC^{SM} mark is a service mark of Northern Virginia Technology Council Inc.

Typically such notes are inserted in small type at the bottom or end of product packaging, advertisements, brochures, and other literature. Adopt a standard practice for insertion of this notice to reduce the chances it will be overlooked or that an infringing party could claim it had no notice of your trademark rights in response to an action you might file against them.

Fair use and comparative advertising

Under recent case law, a party can use another party's marks—even those that are registered—in their descriptive sense to refer descriptively to one's product or services (i.e., not as the name of the product, but to describe an aspect, feature, or function of the product).

Trademark law also permits use of others' marks in comparative advertising, but competitors do not take such uses lightly and could challenge such uses, whether successful or not. Consider (a) whether the other party's product is readily identifiable without use of the trademark, (b) using only so much of the other party's trademark as necessary to identify the product (i.e., name of product versus logo), and (c) whether the intended use creates any likelihood of confusion or suggestion that the other party endorses or sponsors your product or service. Also consider giving appropriate notice to third parties' marks that you use, as recommended for one's own mark above.

Avoid using a mark generically

A mark should never be used in a generic sense. Use of a mark in a generic manner places the mark in the public domain where anyone can use the mark. Xerox had to pay large amounts of money to recapture its Xerox trademark when the word became synonymous with a photocopy.

- Never use the mark as a noun. Rather, use it alone or as an adjective.
- Avoid using testimonials of others when they include use of a mark as a noun.
- What to avoid: "Roller blades are fun to use."
- Proper usage: "Rollerblade® in-line skates offer skaters unique . . ."

Enforcement

Trademark owners should police third parties' use of confusingly similar marks and enforce rights against other uses of confusingly similar marks. The analysis of whether two marks are "confusingly similar" can include as many as 13 factors, depending on the jurisdiction. As a starting point, the analysis can be broken into two parts: (a) whether the marks look or sound similar or have the same meaning; and, if any of these is in the affirmative, (b) whether the goods and services offered under each are likely to be viewed by a reasonable person as coming from the same source. Before challenging another party's use, be careful to confirm that you have superior rights, which in most cases means being sure that you are the prior user.

Domain name disputes and other types of online enforcement

With the proliferation of the online marketplace, one needs to police third parties' use of its marks not only in its own physical backyard, but also online. Trademark rights holders have remedies against those who use their marks (or confusingly similar marks) as domain names (cybersquatters) under the federal Anti-cybersquatting Consumer Protection Act (ACPA, 15 U.S.C. § 1126(d)) and administratively under the Uniform Domain Name Dispute Resolution Policy (UDRP). To prevail under either, the trademark rights holder should be prepared to demonstrate its rights in its mark, the domain name at issue consists of matter that is confusingly similar to the mark, the registrant registered and uses the domain name in bad faith, and the registrant has no right or legitimate interest in the domain name. On the other hand, the registration of a domain name that is similar to one of your trademarks is not actionable if the available content on that domain is not similar to any of your trademarks.

In short, to obtain trademark protection

- Select a mark that fits within your current brand strategy.
- Conduct an availability search to determine whether the proposed use will infringe upon the rights of another. (If a mark also will be a corporate name, conduct a corporate name availability search, which is different than a trademark search.) Also consider domain name availability.
- Register the mark at the federal and state levels.
- Use the mark as registered, maintain the registration, and enforce your rights.
- Consider markets outside the U.S. for similar protection if you currently do, or plan to do, a significant amount of business in those markets.

Notes

Chapter 6

Anatomy of a Patent License

Rick Toering, Womble Carlyle Sandridge & Rice, PLLC

Overview

In general, a patent provides its owner the right to exclude others from making, using, offering to sell, and selling the patented invention in the United States as well as importing the patented invention into the United States. A patent license is typically a contractual relationship between a licensor (patent owner or other patent rights holder) and a licensee whereby the licensor grants certain rights under the patent to the licensee. The following discussion provides a general description of various aspects of the patent license.

What is being licensed?

As the name implies, a patent license typically licenses one or more patents of the licensor to the licensee. Typically, a defined term "licensed patents" is used to define the patents to be licensed, either as a list in the license agreement or as a schedule attached to the license agreement. Often, one or more "future patents" (i.e., pending patent applications that have not yet been granted or in some situations patent applications that have not yet been filed) may be included within the term "licensed patents." Care should be taken when defining "licensed patents" such that neither too many nor too few patents fall within its definition, and in particular so that the term accounts for, as appropriate, future patents.

What activities are permitted by the license?

The patent license typically defines what activities under the licensed patents are permitted. These activities may include the right to make (i.e., manufacture) the patented invention, to have the patented invention made on the licensee's behalf, to sell the patented invention, to use the patented invention, to import the patented invention, or any combination thereof.

For example, distributors, resellers, and/or retailers may be granted the right to sell the patented invention but not the right to manufacture the patented invention. Similarly, a manufacturer may be granted the right to make the patented invention, but not the right to sell the patented invention to another who is not the licensor or the licensor's delegate. In some cases, the licensor may limit the activities in which the licensee is permitted to make, use, or sell the patented invention. Care should be taken when drafting the terms of the license to ensure that neither too few activities nor too many activities are permitted under the license.

How much does the license cost?

A license fee is associated with most, but not necessarily all, patent licenses. The license fee is the mechanism by which the licensor captures a return on the investment made in the development of the technology underlying the licensed patents. The license fee varies widely in its amount and accounting. The license fee may be paid in a single, one-time payment; a time-based payment (e.g., monthly, yearly, etc.); a use-based payment (e.g., number of transactions, number of seats, etc.); or a units-based payment (e.g., number of units sold, number of units manufactured, etc.). The license fee may be expressed in a fixed unit of currency or as a percentage of retail price, wholesale price, profit margin or other such metric. The license fee may vary as a function of use or volume. License fees vary widely and are often industry-specific.Care should be taken when drafting the patent license, because the license fee often becomes a major source of contention between the parties over time.

Is the license exclusive or non-exclusive?

Patent licenses are either exclusive or non-exclusive. In a non-exclusive license, the licensor may grant similar or identical rights under the licensed patents to other licensees. In an exclusive license, the licensee is granted a set of unique rights under the licensed patents and no other party, including the licensor, will have these unique rights. In some cases, exclusive licenses may be limited in certain ways such as limited geographically (e.g., only in the United States, outside the

United States, etc.); limited in time (e.g., for 2 years); or limited to a particular field of use.

Fields of use vary widely and are often used to segregate various markets in relation to the underlying technology. For example, a given technology may have a medical application and a printing application. Each of these applications may constitute a field of use in which the licensor may grant distinct exclusive licenses to different licensees.

Care should be taken when granting exclusive licenses, in particular to ensure that the licensor has a mechanism to change the patent license into a non-exclusive license, such as when licensee fails to fully monetize its rights under the patent license.

Is the license assignable?

Whether a patent license is assignable to another party is sometimes heavily negotiated. A licensee may wish to have the right to assign the patent license to a third party, particularly to effect a sale of some or all of the assets of the licensee's business as purchasers will most times want the necessary rights under the licensed patents to continue to conduct the business. A licensor may not wish to grant the rights to assign the patent license for concern that rights under the licensed patents may end up in the hands of a competitor. Oftentimes, these divergent interests are addressed by permitting the patent license to be assignable with consent of the licensor where such consent is not unreasonably withheld.

Who handles enforcement of the license patents?

Many times a patent license is valuable to a licensee only if the licensed patents are actively policed and enforced. Licensees are typically reluctant to pay license fees if the licensed patents are widely infringed by third parties. Many patent licenses include terms that identify the party (licensor, licensee) that is responsible for enforcing the licensed patents. In many patent licenses, a hybrid approach is adopted whereby one party may elect to enforce the licensed patents and, if not, the other party may elect to enforce the licensed patents. In these hybrid approaches, the party electing to enforce the licensed patents typically controls the enforcement strategy and receives most, if not all, of the proceeds from the enforcement activity.

Who handles prosecution and maintenance of the licensed patents?

Often the licensor controls the prosecution and maintenance of the licensed patents as part of its ordinary course of business. But sometimes, particularly when the technology underlying the licensed patents originates in an educational or governmental institution (i.e., a university or national lab is the owner/licensor), the licensor may require that the licensee bear the expenses associated with the prosecution and maintenance of the licensed patents. In these cases, the licensee may be required to control this activity.

Conclusion

Patent licenses are often necessary tools for business. In many cases, patent licenses allow one party to exploit and commercialize technology developed by another party. Knowing and understanding the key aspects of the patent license allow both parties to achieve a win-win.

SECTION IV
MERGERS AND ACQUISITIONS

CONTENTS

Chapter 1

Structuring a Business Acquisition

David J. Charles, Pillsbury Winthrop Shaw Pittman LLP

Introduction

There are many ways to structure the acquisition of a business. The ideal structure for any particular transaction depends on a number of considerations, including, among others: (i) the type of acquiring entity, such as a corporation, limited liability company (LLC), or partnership; (ii) the type of target, such a corporation, LLC, partnership, or unincorporated division; (iii) the nature and scope of the target's business operations, including types of commercial relationships, liability risks, and regulatory matters; (iv) the desired tax results; and (v) the composition of the proposed consideration for the transaction, whether cash, stock, or a combination thereof.

This chapter discusses the basic structures that are used by private corporations to acquire businesses.

Asset purchase

In an asset purchase transaction, the buyer acquires the assets of target company from a seller and assumes only specified liabilities related to the operations of the target company for the specified consideration.

An asset purchase transaction can be used to acquire any type of legally recognized entity, but as a practical matter will almost always be used to acquire a target company that is an unincorporated division of the seller or a target company that has significant liabilities (actual or potential) for which a buyer will not agree to assume any risk. Note that under certain circumstances, a buyer will succeed to all of the liabilities of a target company as a result of an asset purchase, notwithstanding the fact that the transaction expressly excludes those liabilities.

An asset purchase can be structured as tax deferred or taxable, depending on the composition of the consideration and the tax status of the buyer and target company. If, among other technical requirements, the buyer and target company are corporations for tax purposes, voting capital stock of the buyer constitutes at least 80 percent of the consideration paid for the target company assets, substantially all of the assets of the target company are transferred to the buyer, and the target company liquidates in connection with the transaction, the transaction may qualify for tax deferred treatment.

If an asset purchase is a taxable transaction, the buyer will allocate the purchase price to the target company assets being acquired, thus generating depreciation and amortization deductions that will inure to its benefit after the closing if the target company has built-in gain in its assets.

In order to effect an asset purchase transaction:

- The seller will generally have to obtain consents from third parties to asset transfer, subjecting the transaction to execution/closing risk based on whether third parties grant their consent; and
- if the target company business is a going concern, the seller will have to terminate the employees engaged in the target company business and the buyer will have to rehire them, triggering various costs, including any applicable severance payments.

An asset purchase cannot be used if the target company business operates in a regulated industry and the required licenses and/or permits are not, by their terms, transferrable, unless the buyer has its own authorizations that cover the target company business.

Stock purchase

In a stock purchase transaction, the buyer acquires issued and outstanding shares of capital stock in the target company from the seller for the specified consideration.

A stock purchase is used to acquire a target company that is a legally recognized entity. Note that the transaction will be styled as a "membership interest purchase" or "unit purchase" if the target company is an LLC.

As a result of a stock purchase transaction involving all of the stock of the target company, the target company becomes a wholly owned subsidiary of the buyer.

A stock purchase transaction can be structured as tax deferred or taxable, depending on the tax status of the buyer and target company and the composition of the consideration. If, among other technical requirements, the target company and buyer are both corporations and the only consideration paid for the equity in the target company is the buyer voting capital stock, the transaction may qualify for tax deferred treatment. As a general matter, the buyer will acquire a basis in the stock of the target company equal to the purchase price for the transaction if it is a taxable stock purchase. If a stock purchase is a taxable transaction, the buyer is a corporation for tax purposes, and the target company is either an S corporation for tax purposes or a corporate subsidiary, and other technical requirements are satisfied, the buyer and seller may make a special election under applicable tax rules to treat the transaction as an asset purchase, allowing the buyer to allocate the purchase price to the assets of the target company, thus generating deductions that will inure to its benefit after the closing if the target company has built-in gain in its assets.

Generally, stock purchase transactions trigger few third-party consent requirements.

Merger

Direct Merger
In a direct merger transaction, the target company merges with and into the buyer, and the seller receives the specified consideration.

A direct merger can be used to acquire a target company that is a legally recognized entity.

A direct merger transaction can be structured as tax deferred or taxable, depending on the tax status of the buyer and target company and the composition of the consideration. If, among other technical requirements, the buyer and target company are corporations for tax purposes and capital stock of the buyer constitutes at least 40 percent of the consideration paid to the seller in connection with the merger, the transaction may qualify for tax deferred treatment.

As a result of a direct merger transaction, the target company ceases to exist as a separate entity, and the buyer succeeds to all of the assets, liabilities, franchises, and powers of the target company. Because the target company ceases to exist, the transaction typically triggers third-party consents.

Subsidiary Merger

In a subsidiary merger transaction, the target company merges with a subsidiary of the buyer, and the seller receives the specified consideration. A subsidiary merger transaction can be structured as "forward," which means the target company merges with and into the subsidiary of the buyer, and the subsidiary of the buyer survives the merger; or as "reverse," which means that the subsidiary of the buyer merges with and into the target company, and the target company survives the merger.

A subsidiary merger can be used to acquire a target company that is a legally recognized entity.

A subsidiary merger transaction can be structured as tax deferred or taxable, depending on the tax status of the buyer and target company and the composition of the consideration. If, among other technical requirements, capital stock of the buyer constitutes at least 40 percent of the consideration paid to the seller in connection with a "forward" subsidiary merger, and substantially all of the assets of the target company are acquired in the merger, the transaction may qualify for tax deferred treatment. If, among other technical requirements, capital stock of the buyer constitutes at least 80 percent of the consideration paid to the seller in connection with a "reverse" subsidiary merger, and substantially all of the target company's assets are retained in connection with the merger, the transaction may qualify for tax deferred treatment.

As a result of a "forward" subsidiary merger transaction, the target company ceases to exist as a separate entity and the subsidiary of the buyer succeeds to all of the assets, liabilities, franchises, and powers of the target company. Because the target company ceases to exist, the transaction typically triggers third-party consents. As a result of a "reverse" subsidiary merger transaction, the target company continues in existence, so the transaction typically triggers fewer third-party consents.

Conclusion

A business acquisition transaction can be structured in different ways, depending on the nature of the buyer and the target, as well as specific business objectives (including tax considerations).

Internal Revenue Service regulations generally provide that, for the purpose of avoiding federal tax penalties, a taxpayer may rely only on formal written advice meeting specific requirements. The tax advice in this document does not meet those requirements. Accordingly, the tax advice was not intended or written to be used, and it cannot be used, for the purpose of avoiding federal tax penalties that may be imposed on you.

Notes

Chapter 2

Timeline for a Business Acquisition

David J. Charles, Pillsbury Winthrop Shaw Pittman LLP

While business acquisitions may take different forms, they generally proceed according to the following timeline.

Identify target

All business acquisitions commence with the identification of a suitable target. Targets are identified either as a result of a buyer's internal business development efforts or in connection with a sale process run by an investment banker or business broker. Investment bankers and business brokers typically use a 1- to 2-page "teaser" that describes the target without disclosing its name to generate interest in the opportunity.

Enter into confidentiality/non-disclosure agreement

After a potential buyer expresses a general interest in a target opportunity, the parties will enter into a confidentiality or non-disclosure agreement that governs the exchange of material non-public information between them during the entire acquisition process. Confidentiality or non-disclosure agreements are not usually subject to much negotiation, and often agreed to "as is" or with few modifications.

Obtain offering/information memorandum

If an investment banker or business broker is running a sale process for a particular target, the banker or broker circulates an offering or information memorandum once a confidentiality or non-disclosure agreement is in place. The offering or information memorandum is strictly confidential and contains a detailed description of the target company, including historical and summary financial information. The purpose of the offering or information memorandum is to provide potential buyers with sufficient information so that they can make a decision about whether to proceed with the transaction and formulate a valuation for the target.

Submit indication of interest (IOI)

After considering the offering or information memorandum, prospective buyers that are interested in an opportunity presented by an investment banker or business broker are asked to submit indications of interest (IOIs). The IOI generally confirms the buyer's interest in the opportunity at a particular price level or price range. The investment banker or business broker uses the IOIs to differentiate the potential buyers based on their valuations of the target opportunity and to focus the transaction effort on the strongest offers.

Conduct preliminary due diligence

Generally, only the buyers who indicate competitive offers in their IOIs are afforded the opportunity to conduct preliminary due diligence at this point. The preliminary due diligence is intended to enable the buyers that are down-selected to prepare reasonably specific acquisition proposals.

As part of the preliminary due diligence, buyers are generally afforded the opportunity to receive management presentations about the target company and access to additional financial, tax, and accounting information, as well as certain contracts, documents, and business records. This information is often made available to potential buyers through a virtual dataroom that is only accessible online.

Enter into letter of intent/exclusivity agreement

Buyers that are interested in pursuing a target after having conducted preliminary due diligence are typically required to submit a detailed letter of intent (LOI) and exclusivity agreement at this stage in the process. The investment banker or business broker sets a hard deadline for submission of LOIs from the prospective buyers. The LOI contains specific information about each potential buyer's acquisition proposal, including price, transaction structure, and material conditions to closing.

Sellers generally have the most leverage at this point in the process, so it is beneficial for them to negotiate as many specific, material transaction terms or conditions as possible. Buyers tend to push for LOIs with meaningful exclusivity periods (60 to 90 days) so that they can invest the necessary resources to pursue a transaction without the fear of another buyer "topping" them. LOIs are often reviewed, negotiated, and finalized within 1 to 3 weeks.

Conduct full legal and business due diligence

A buyer will conduct full legal and business due diligence on a target company once an LOI with a meaningful exclusivity period is entered into. During this stage, the buyer will seek access to all of the target company's financial, legal, accounting, and tax information, as well as the essential business documents and records, including the target company's formation documents and minute books, customer contracts, supplier contracts, loan documents, office leases, equipment leases, software licenses, employment agreements, benefit plans, employee handbooks/manuals, and regulatory filings.

In connection with this review, a buyer will generally deliver a detailed due diligence request list that identifies specific items. These lists tend to be long (10 to 20 pages) and should be tailored to the specific target company, given the nature of its business. Additional materials are generally made available to the buyer in response to its due diligence request list by being posted in a virtual dataroom.

This review is intended to confirm all of the information about the target company made available to the buyer up to this point and the buyer's assumptions about the target company that support its valuation of the target company as presented in the LOI, as well as to identify legal or business risks associated with the potential acquisition. As a general matter, a buyer will not have access to a target company's customers or employees until the definitive acquisition document is complete (or nearly complete).

Negotiate definitive acquisition document

Once an LOI is signed, a buyer will typically begin preparing an initial draft of the definitive acquisition agreement. Many buyers are reluctant to circulate a draft purchase agreement until they have received initial findings from their full legal and business due diligence review. Most buyers will, however, dual-track negotiating the definitive acquisition documentation and conducting their full legal and business due diligence.

Drafting and negotiating a definitive acquisition agreement is a process that necessarily requires input from the buyer/seller and their financial, accounting, tax, and legal advisors. While most acquisition agreements use a similar architecture, every purchase document contains terms and conditions that are unique to that transaction. Section IV, Chapter 3: Anatomy of a Business Acquisition Agreement, outlines the basic structure for a business acquisition agreement. Generally, the due diligence review and definitive acquisition document takes more than three-fourths of the total effort required to complete an acquisition, from the buyer's perspective.

Satisfy conditions to closing

After a definitive purchase agreement is completed, the parties will immediately focus their attention on satisfying the conditions precedent for the closing. The acquisition agreement specifies the actions that need to be taken by each party before the closing can occur (including the various documents, certificates, consents, and approvals that must be delivered). The parties necessarily cooperate with each other to cause these conditions to closing to be satisfied as promptly as possible.

Close transaction

Once the conditions to closing are satisfied, the parties will close the transaction. Closings are conducted remotely, with documents, certificates, consents, and approvals being exchanged electronically or by overnight mail/Federal Express. "Ceremonial" and/or in person closings are increasingly rare.

Conclusion

All members of a transaction team (buy-side and sell-side) should understand the specific timeline for the business acquisition.

ço   ço   ço

Chapter 3

Anatomy of a Business Acquisition Agreement

David J. Charles, Pillsbury Winthrop Shaw Pittman LLP

Nearly all agreements for the acquisition of a private business have the same basic architecture. Whether the target is a corporation, limited liability company, partnership, or operating division, and however the transaction is structured (taxable or tax-deferred, stock/membership purchase, asset purchase or merger), the definitive document will have core terms and conditions that are essentially the same and operate together in a similar fashion. These terms and conditions are typically grouped into "articles" that have "sections" and "subsections." This chapter provides an overview of the core provisions that appear in nearly every M&A agreement where the target is a private business.

Preamble and recitals

Business acquisition agreements always start with a preamble and recitals. The preamble identifies the type of agreement, the parties to the transaction, and date of the agreement. The recitals (sometimes styled as "whereas" clauses) describe the relationships of the parties and the parties' general intentions for the transaction. Sometimes, the recitals also provide key definitions that are used throughout the body of the agreement. The following are the preamble and recitals from the definitive agreement used by NCI Information Systems Inc. to acquire Karta Technologies Inc. (which was filed with the SEC in June 2007):

THIS STOCK PURCHASE AGREEMENT (this "Agreement") is entered into as of the 27th day of June, 2007, by and among NCI Information Systems, Inc., a Virginia corporation (Purchaser), Karta Technologies, Inc., a Texas corporation (Company), those Persons listed on Schedule 1A hereto (collectively, "Sellers"), Parvinder Kaur (Special Indemnitor), and Gurvinder Pal Singh, as representative of all of the Sellers and the Special Indemnitor (the "Representative").

RECITALS

A. Sellers collectively own all of the issued and outstanding capital stock of Company, consisting of 10,250,000 shares of Common Stock, par value $0.01 per share (the "Company Stock").

B. Sellers desire to sell and convey the Company Stock to Purchaser, and Purchaser desires to purchase the Company Stock from Sellers, upon the terms and conditions set forth in this Agreement.

Article 1—The transaction

In most M&A agreements, the first article describes the transaction in detail, defines the purchase price, and indicates how the purchase price is to be paid. If there are escrows, deferred payments, or contingent/earn-out payments, these will be included in this article. Often, this article also establishes a date, time, and place for the closing.

Article 2—Representations and warranties regarding the sellers

This article includes specific statements by the sellers, generally limited to factual and legal matters about the sellers that underpin the basic transaction. For example, this article includes representations and warranties that the sellers have the power, authority, and capacity to execute and deliver the acquisition agreement and perform their respective obligations under the agreement, and that such conduct will not violate any laws governing the sellers or breach any agreements binding on them.

Article 3—Representations and warranties regarding the target

This article includes specific statements about the target that cover broad legal, business, and operational matters, and is typically the longest part of an agreement, often constituting one-fourth to one-half of the entire document. Sometimes, the representations and warranties about the sellers and the target business are combined into a single article. The representations and warranties about the target serve dual purposes of disclosure and risk allocation. The scope of a particular representation or warranty may be qualified to the "knowledge" of the party making it and/or by the term "material" (or a specific dollar threshold), which has the correlative effect of limiting or expanding the parties' indemnification rights and obligations for matters that arise or are discovered after the closing. The following section from the definitive agreement used by Perot Systems Corporation to acquire Soza & Co., Ltd. (which was filed with the SEC in March 2003) illustrates the dual purposes served by representations and warranties and how they can be qualified:

> 2.17 Permits. The Companies own or possess all right, title and interest in all material permits, licenses, authorizations, approvals, quality certifications, franchises, or rights issued by any Governmental Body necessary to conduct their business as currently conducted (collectively, "Permits"). Each Permit is listed on Schedule 2.17. No loss or expiration of any Permit on Schedule 2.17 will result from the transactions contemplated by this Agreement and no loss or expiration of any Permit on Schedule 2.17 is otherwise, pending or, to Sellers' Knowledge, threatened other than the expiration of such Permits in accordance with their terms that may be renewed in the Ordinary Course of Business without lapsing.

In response to this representation, the sellers had to disclose all of the target company's material (but not immaterial) permits. The buyer then used this list to confirm the findings of its due diligence review. Further, this section puts the risk of a material permit being cancelled as a result of the transaction on the sellers.

The various lists called for by the representations and warranties regarding the target business, as well as any exceptions to such representations and warranties that are necessary to make them correct, are always compiled and presented as "disclosure schedules" to the M&A agreement.

Article 4—Representations and warranties regarding the buyer

This article includes specific statements by the buyer, generally limited to factual and legal matters about the buyer that underpin the basic transaction. For example, this article includes representations and warranties that the buyer has the power and authority to execute and deliver the acquisition agreement and perform its obligations under the agreement, that such conduct will not violate any laws governing the buyer or breach any agreements binding on the buyer, and that the buyer has (or will have as of the closing) sufficient cash to pay the portion of the purchase price that is due at the closing.

If the transaction includes deferred payments or contingent/earn-out payments, this article will have additional representations and warranties that are designed to protect the sellers' ability to realize these.

Article 5—Pre-closing covenants

This article imposes obligations and limitations on actions by the target company and the sellers between the date the purchase agreement is signed and the closing of the transaction. This article always includes a list of specific actions related to the operation of the business that the target company and the sellers are precluded from taking during the "gap" period. These restrictions are designed to protect the integrity of the target business the buyer has agreed to purchase.

This article almost always includes an "exclusivity" or "non-solicitation" section that expressly precludes the target and its owners from seeking or accepting a competing offer. It also describes those matters on which the parties will cooperate between signing and closing, including efforts to obtain third-party consents and approvals triggered by the transaction.

Article 6—Conditions precedent to closing

This article establishes the various benchmarks that trigger the parties' respective obligations to consummate the transaction. It lists, with specificity, what each party has to deliver or produce (e.g., cash, closing certificates, stock certificates, business records, director/officer resignations, consent letters, regulatory approvals, and ancillary agreements, if any), and what events must occur (or fail to have occurred), in order to require the other parties to close the deal.

These "conditions precedent" must be either "waived" by the party for whose benefit they operate or "satisfied" by the other party (or a third party or external event) before a closing can occur. Some M&A agreements expressly state that the conditions precedent are waived if a party consummates the closing, meaning that party cannot bring a claim after the closing based on the fact that a particular condition precedent was never satisfied.

Article 7—Termination

This article includes the terms and conditions under which the parties may terminate the agreement and the consequences of such termination.

Article 8—Post-closing covenants

This article describes how the parties will conduct themselves after the closing vis-à-vis each other, with respect to matters that concern the acquisition. It typically includes a section on "further assurances," pursuant to which each party agrees to take such reasonable actions as another party may request in order to effect the overall transaction, and a section requiring reasonable cooperation with respect to ongoing litigation or governmental investigations. It will include additional covenants and agreements regarding how the buyer will operate the target business after the closing if the transaction includes contingent/earn-out payments in order to protect the sellers' ability to realize these.

Article 9—Indemnification

This article establishes the procedures and standards for both claims between or among the parties arising under the definitive agreement for breaches of representations and warranties, failures to perform covenants, and liabilities that are identified (either specifically or generally) as of the signing, and certain claims by third parties directed against the target business.

Although this article usually constitutes less than 10 percent of the entire agreement, it frequently receives more than 90 percent of the attention during negotiation. The key provisions in this article seek to limit the parties' indemnification obligations and relate to the duration (or "survival" period) of each party's representations and warranties, and corresponding indemnification obligations; whether and to what extent indemnification claims will be subject to a deductible or minimum claim (sometimes referred to as either a "threshold" or "basket") before a party has to pay money to another party;

each party's maximum exposure for indemnification claims (the "cap"); and those specific types of claims, if any, that are excluded from these limitations (the "carve-outs"). The following sections from the definitive agreement used by ManTech International Corporation to acquire CTX Corporation (which was filed with the SEC in December 2002) illustrates how indemnification obligations can be limited:

Section 7.3 Survival of Representations and Warranties; Limitations on Indemnification.

(a) Survival. The representations and warranties in this Agreement, and the indemnification obligations in this Agreement with respect thereto, shall survive the Closing for a period of one (1) year following the Closing Date, at which time they shall terminate and no claim shall thereafter be brought in respect of them; provided, however, that such termination shall not affect any claim for breach of any representation or warranty if written notice thereof, in reasonable detail, has been given to the breaching party prior to such termination date (in such case, the survival period for such representation and warranty shall continue solely with respect to such claim until the claim is fully resolved). The covenants of the parties set forth in this Agreement to be performed after the Closing shall survive until performed.

(b) Limitation on Indemnification. Notwithstanding anything else in this Agreement to the contrary, (i) none of Buyer, Merger Sub nor any of Buyer's Affiliates shall make any claim against the Escrow Participants for any Losses described in Section 7.1 until the Buyer, Merger Sub or Buyer's Affiliates have suffered, incurred, sustained or become subject to such Losses in excess of Two Hundred and Seventy Five Thousand Dollars ($275,000) (the "Deductible Amount"), (ii) if such Deductible Amount is exceeded, the Escrow Participants shall be required to pay to the indemnified parties, solely from the Indemnification Escrow Account, only the amount by which the aggregate of such Losses exceeds the Deductible Amount (the "Indemnified Losses"); and (iii) the obligation and liability for any and all Indemnified Losses and any other indemnification set forth in this Agreement of each Escrow Participant shall not, in any event, exceed such Escrow Participant's portion of the Closing Merger Consideration that is withheld pursuant to Section 2.7(e).

The following section from the definitive agreement used by Veridian Corporation to acquire Signal Corporation (which was filed with the SEC in September 2002) includes even more detailed limitations on the sellers' indemnification obligations, such as a "mini basket" to insulate the sellers from liability for "small" claims, and provides for specific "carve-outs" from the limitations:

8.4 LIMITATIONS ON SELLERS' INDEMNIFICATION OBLIGATIONS.

8.4.1 Sellers shall not be liable to the Purchaser Indemnitees with respect to any Claim for indemnification under Section 8.3 unless (i) the amount of Damages resulting from any separate fact, condition or event that constitutes a Breach of a representation or warranty relating to such Claim is in excess of $50,000 (the "Individual Indemnification Threshold") and (ii) the aggregate amount of Damages relating to Claims meeting the Individual Indemnification Threshold (but excluding any claims for which the thresholds in this Section 8.4.1 do not apply) is in excess of $1,250,000 (the "Aggregate Indemnification Threshold"). Once the Aggregate Indemnification Threshold has been met, Sellers shall then be liable for all Claims in excess of the Individual Indemnification Threshold excluding such Claims as were aggregated to reach the Aggregate Indemnification Threshold. Notwithstanding the foregoing, Sellers shall be liable for all Claims arising under Sections 8.3.3, 8.3.4 and 8.3.5 and Breaches of Section 2.4.12 and Section 10.5, without regard to the Individual Indemnification Threshold or Aggregate Indemnification Threshold.

8.4.2 The maximum amount for which Sellers shall be liable to the Purchaser Indemnitees under this Agreement or any Transaction Document, and for the transactions described herein, is $20,000,000 (the "Indemnification Limit"); provided, that, neither Seller shall be liable to the Purchaser Indemnitees, in the aggregate, under this Agreement, and for the transactions described herein, for more than his or her Pro Rata Portion of the Indemnification Limit; and provided, further, that neither Seller shall be liable to any Purchaser Indemnitee with respect to any individual Claim for indemnification under Section 8.3 for more than his or her Pro Rata Portion of the amount that is finally determined to be due and owing to such Purchaser Indemnitee. Notwithstanding the foregoing, the Indemnification Limit shall not apply to Claims arising under Sections 8.3.3, 8.3.4 and 8.3.5 and Breaches of Section 2.4.12 and Sections 10.1, 10.2 and 10.5, nor shall such Claims be counted toward the Indemnification Limit.

8.4.3 Sellers' representations and warranties, and Sellers' obligation to indemnify the Purchaser Indemnitees under Section 8.3, shall survive the Closing and will remain in effect until: (i) February 15, 2004 with respect to any failure on the part of Sellers or the SIGNAL Companies to perform any covenants or agreements set forth herein, or any Breach of any of the representations and warranties made in Article 2, other than such representations and warranties specifically identified in the following clause; (ii) sixty (60) days after the expiration of the applicable federal or state statute of limitations, whichever is longer, with respect to any Breach of any of the representations and warranties made in Sections 2.4 or 2.9 or Damages described in Sections 8.3.3; or (iii) four years and 180 days from the Closing Date with respect to the Damages described in Section 8.3.4. Notwithstanding the foregoing, Sellers' representations and warranties made in Sections 2.2.1, 2.2.10, 2.2.11, 2.4.12, Sellers' covenants in Sections 10.1, 10.2 and 10.5 and Sellers' obligation to indemnify the Purchaser Indemnities for any Breach of these representations, warranties and covenant under Section 8.3, as well as Sellers' obligation to indemnify the Purchaser Indemnities under Section 8.3.5 shall survive indefinitely.

Article 10—Tax matters

Most agreements for the acquisition of a private business will have a separate article dedicated to tax matters that describes the parties' rights and obligations after the closing with respect to filing tax returns, amending tax returns, satisfying tax liabilities that become due and payable after the closing, processing refund claims, and dealing with tax audits.

Article 11—Miscellaneous

The last article of an M&A agreement typically contains more general, legal provisions, such as the requirements and procedures for official communications (or "notices) under the agreement, the law that governs the agreement, how the agreement may be amended or modified, and rules for interpreting or construing the agreement, that are often described as "boilerplate." This article frequently receives the least attention during the drafting and negotiation process, but should not be overlooked, as it includes substantive business provisions (for example, sections allocating liability for transaction fees and expenses) in many M&A agreements.

Conclusion

Senior executives involved in M&A transactions should be familiar with the basic architecture used for business acquisition agreements.

SECTION V
DECIDING WHETHER TO GO PUBLIC

CONTENTS

Chapter 1

Deciding Whether To Go Public

Curtis L. Schehr, DCS, Manik K. Rath, and Tamara Jack, LMI

Going public is one of the most critical decisions a company can make and should be evaluated thoughtfully with a full understanding of the many pros and cons. This chapter outlines some of the benefits, disadvantages, and other considerations associated with taking a company public. As with most significant business matters, deciding whether to go public should involve an intensive level of analysis and corporate introspection that considers both objective and subjective factors.

Benefits of going public

Cash to support company's growth strategy

Among the frequently cited benefits of going public is raising funds for the company's growth. The company's growth strategy could involve investing in technology, infrastructure improvements, hiring additional or more talented employees, or some combination of the foregoing. The company might also use the offering proceeds to reduce its outstanding debt and provide working capital to support ongoing operations. Identifying sound, constructive uses for the cash raised from an IPO is typically non-controversial.

Liquidity for investors and employees

Going public also creates a liquid market for the company's pre-IPO investors, which may include employees. Once public, the company's stockholders have an easily accessible market through which they have the opportunity (in some instances with restrictions) to monetize some or potentially all of the appreciated value of their equity stake in the company. The enhanced liquidity offered by a publicly traded company stands in marked contrast to the relative difficulty a stockholder in a privately held company faces in realizing any gain from the increased value of his or her investment. It should be noted, however, that the underwriters typically require a newly public company's executive management and directors to be subject to a "lock-up" period of 180 days following the IPO during which they may not trade in the company's stock.

Enhanced employee recruitment and retention

Another benefit of being publicly traded involves the company's increased ability to attract, hire, and retain employees. Effective use of a public company's equity compensation plan can be a powerful tool that motivates and guides employee behavior toward the objectives identified by executive management and the board. Additionally, the company may decide to implement a broad-based employee stock purchase plan that facilitates the purchase of company stock at a discount to the market and enables ownership across the entire employee population.

Acquisition currency

Publicly traded companies engaging in mergers and acquisitions as part of their growth strategy have the flexibility to use company stock as part of the purchase consideration in lieu of cash. In fact, the acquisition of a target company's stock using the acquiring company's shares may be eligible for favorable tax treatment that would not apply if the acquisition were cash-based. Of course, the shares issued by a company in connection with an acquisition will typically need to be registered with the SEC in order to be freely tradable.

Increased market value and access to additional capital

Proponents of going public often point to the fact that the market value of a publicly traded company relative to a comparable private company is typically higher because of the liquidity and prestige associated with a public company. Additionally, a public company may decide to undertake follow on offerings of company stock to raise additional cash. Such follow on offerings are significantly more streamlined than an IPO in terms of timetable and cost, since much of the groundwork has already been laid with the registration statement and other IPO documents previously filed with the SEC. A company must be public for at least 12 months before it can register shares for a follow on offering.

Disadvantages of going public

Company decisions and actions that are maintained confidential while the company is private may need to be disclosed once the company is public. Management's decisions are subject to potentially significant scrutiny. The analogy of "living in a fish bowl" is an apt descriptor of executive management life running a public company. Most important, perhaps, is recognizing the potential liability directors and officers face under federal securities laws when a company decides to access the securities markets. The imperative of fully complying at all times with the myriad disclosure obligations imposed by federal securities laws and regulations cannot be overemphasized.

Management distraction

Management will be significantly distracted from running the business before and after the IPO, with the CEO, CFO, general counsel, and their respective staffs devoting an appreciable amount of attention to the requirements of being publicly traded. The IPO process will typically take 3 to 6 months and include due diligence activities; preparing, reviewing, and filing the SEC registration statement (Form S-1); and a "road-show" by the CEO and CFO—a typically grueling, several-week marathon of presentations by the CEO and CFO—to market the offering to prospective investors.

Compliance with SEC and exchange listing requirements is demanding

Compliance with SEC rules and the standards of the stock exchange on which the company is listed (NYSE or NASDAQ) is a significant undertaking. A public company is required, among other things, to file quarterly reports (Form 10-Q), an annual report (Form 10-K), current reports (Form 8-K) to announce specific events, and a proxy statement in connection with the annual meeting of stockholders. The company will be required to periodically disclose a wide range of information not only about the company's business, financial condition, and results of operations, but also about its executive officers, directors, and board committees, executive compensation, director fees, stock-based compensation plans, and governance practices.

Sarbanes-Oxley Act compliance is onerous and costly

The passage of the Sarbanes-Oxley Act of 2002 (SOX) added a significant level of complexity to being public. SOX was adopted in the wake of numerous scandals involving corporate malfeasance at the highest levels involving companies such as Enron, WorldCom (MCI), Adelphia, and Tyco. The law emphasizes increased transparency by companies and requires significantly more expansive and prompt disclosure of information to shareholders and the public.

One of the most controversial provisions of SOX is Section 404, under which companies and their independent public accounting firms are required to test and report on the adequacy of the company's internal controls over financial reporting. Section 404 requires each public company's annual report to contain (1) a statement of management's responsibility for establishing and maintaining an adequate internal control structure and procedures for financial reporting; and (2) management's assessment, as of the end of each fiscal year, of the effectiveness of the company's internal control structure and procedures for financial reporting. Section 404 also requires the company's auditor to attest to, and report on management's assessment of, the effectiveness of the company's internal controls and procedures for financial reporting in accordance with standards established by the Public Company Accounting Oversight Board. The potential difficulty and cost of bringing a private company's internal controls over financial reporting (from a design, documentation, and implementation standpoint) to the level necessary to adequately satisfy SOX Section 404 is significant.

SOX also mandates that the CEO and CFO make two substantive certifications in each annual and quarterly report filed with the SEC. While the substance and potential ramifications of these two certifications goes beyond the scope of this chapter, the potential sanctions for false certification are severe. Companies that go public have a grace period (until their second annual report) before being required to comply with SOX 404.

Disclosure of executive compensation
Executive compensation is one of the principal areas targeted in recent years by the SEC and other interested parties for enhanced transparency and disclosure. For example, transactions involving the company's stock—including derivatives such as stock options or restricted stock units—by the most highly compensated executives, including the CEO and CFO, are required to be publicly filed with the SEC within 2 business days of such transaction. Additionally, the company and compensation committee of the board are required to describe in SEC filings the company's compensation philosophy, incentive plans (both cash and equity based), and related grant decisions. Moreover, for the CEO, CFO, and three most highly compensated executive officers—collectively referred to as "Named Executive Officers"—the company is required to publicly disclose detailed information on the cash, equity, benefits, and other perquisites that comprise their total compensation packages.

Be careful what you say and to whom
Management in a publicly traded company also has to be particularly mindful of Regulation Fair Disclosure (Reg. FD), which generally prohibits selective disclosure

of material, non-public information to securities market professionals and holders of the company's securities. The SEC has been increasingly aggressive in pursuing violations of Reg. FD. CEO and CFO meetings with analysts and the media, as well as public speaking appearances, need to be approached with extreme caution. The impacts of violating Reg. FD are both financial and reputational. The pitfalls of Reg. FD are sometimes overshadowed by the potential liability associated with insider trading and the emphasis on implementing company policies, procedures, and training to foster compliance in that area.

Going and staying public is expensive
Going public is expensive, when one adds up the legal, outside auditor, printer, transfer agent fees, and filing costs. In addition, the annual recurring costs of being public are substantial. Director and officer insurance for public companies is significantly more expensive than such insurance for a comparably sized private company. The difference is principally because of the increased probability of (and settlement values associated with) shareholder class actions alleging securities fraud and other claims.

Now that you've decided to go public

Assemble your advisors
Assuming your company has decided to move forward with the process of preparing for an IPO, the company will need, among other things, to assemble a team of experienced advisors, including attorneys, outside auditors, and investment bankers. This team should be well prepared to guide the company through the preparatory and execution phases of the process. The fees charged by the company's advisors, along with regulatory filing fees, are significant and usually paid out of the proceeds of the IPO.

Director independence and corporate governance requirements
NYSE, NASDAQ, and SEC rules and regulations have certain requirements affecting the composition of the board of directors and its committees. Public company boards must have a majority of independent directors. Audit committees of the board are required to have at least three directors who meet certain financial literacy requirements, and one of the three audit committee directors must satisfy the fairly stringent SEC definition of an Audit Committee Financial Expert. Depending on whether your company intends to list on the NYSE or NASDAQ, the independence requirements for directors serving on other board committees such as compensation and nominating vary somewhat. Determining whether a

director is independent involves a rule—and fact-based assessment that should be undertaken with the assistance of experienced legal counsel.

Depending on the composition of your company's board pre-IPO, the board may need to undertake certain restructuring actions to meet the independence requirements. Although the NYSE, NASDAQ, and SEC provide phase-in periods for newly public companies to comply with the director independence requirements, it is highly advisable for the company's board and board committees to meet the requirements on or before the date of the public offering.

Due diligence

The investment banking firms that serve as firm commitment underwriters and their counsel, as well as the company's counsel, will perform a detailed fact-finding review of the company's corporate records, financial statements, policies and procedures, and contingency and risk issues, and will examine the company's business pipeline. The purpose of the review is to ensure the accuracy and completeness of the information in the registration statement to be filed by the company with the SEC. Due diligence is particularly important to the company's outside advisors, officers, and directors because, if done correctly, it provides a potential defense against liability under federal securities laws for a misleading registration statement.

The "C suite" team

The CEO and company's board of directors should assess whether the company has the requisite experience and talent in the "C suite" to run a public company. In addition to the CEO, the company's chief financial officer and general counsel are critical players, as is a solid investor relations manager. The CEO and CFO will have the most face time with securities analysts and institutional investors and must be able to tell the company's story concisely and persuasively, both for purposes of the road show to market the offering and to deal effectively with investors and analysts post-IPO. It is vital that the CEO and CFO establish credibility with Wall Street from the outset, considering the significant impact that such credibility can have on the company's stock price.

Remember that speed can be dangerous

There will be constant, intense pressure from the investment bankers and others to move quickly to complete the IPO once the decision to proceed is made. While there are many sound reasons to move expeditiously, it is imperative that the accuracy and completeness of the registration statement and other material documents not be compromised on the altar of speed. Additionally, the company's board of directors, a majority of whom are required to sign the registration statement, must be kept adequately informed by management and counsel at key stages throughout the process. While all stakeholders in the IPO process share the objective of completing the offering promptly, the adverse consequences of a flawed offering will be substantially more far-reaching than the effect of taking the necessary time to do things right the first time. In this regard, the company's executive team and board should retain and exercise the final say when it comes to the elasticity of the IPO timetable.

Notes

SECTION VI
GOVERNMENT CONTRACTS

CONTENTS

Chapter 1

Top Things To Know About Government Contract Formation

Kevin T. Boyle, Vangent, Inc., J. Scott Hommer, III, and
Justin J. Wortman, Venable LLP

Contracting with the federal government can be roughly divided into two fundamental aspects: contract formation and contract administration. In order to understand contract formation, it is important to understand the law that controls the formation of contracts, the different types of contracts available to the government, and the different methods of procurement the government uses. This chapter provides an overview of these topics.

1. What regulations control the formation of government contracts?

The Federal Acquisition Regulation (the "FAR):

1. Sets forth policies and procedures for acquisitions by all executive agencies. The Federal Aviation Administration, United States Postal Service, legislative, and judicial branches maintain their own procurement procedures.
2. Is codified at Title 48 of the Code of Federal Regulations.

While the FAR is the primary document, each agency may—and most often do—adopt acquisition regulations that supplement the FAR.

The FAR and Agency Supplements to the FAR include standard solicitation provisions and contract clauses.

Almost no deviations from standard FAR clauses are allowed during contract formation.

1. The FAR states, for example, that "[i]ndividual deviations affect only one contract action, and . . . may be authorized by the agency head." FAR 1.403.
2. But under FAR Part 12—Commercial Item Acquisition—contracting officers may "tailor" clauses to a particular procurement. (The term "commercial item" is defined by the FAR to include, among other things, any item, other than real property, that is of a type customarily used by the general public or by non-governmental entities for purposes other than governmental purposes, and has been offered or actually sold, leased, or licensed to the general public.)
3. To challenge the inclusion of a clause in a solicitation, an offeror must protest the terms of a solicitation prior to bidding.

2. What are the types of contracts the federal government can use?

The federal government uses a number of types of contracts that vary based on how the contractor will be paid for its performance.

1. Cost-reimbursement: Under this type of contract, a contractor is reimbursed by the government for all of its allowed expenses in performing work under the contract. Cost reimbursement contracts typically contain either a fixed fee or award fee component that provides an element of profit to the contractor.
2. Fixed-price: Under this type of contract, the contractor is paid a negotiated fixed-price for timely delivery of an item or service.
3. Incentive-based: These contracts fall somewhere between cost-reimbursement and fixed-price. The government encourages a contractor to keep costs down by allowing the company to share a portion of the savings.
4. Time and materials: The government uses this type of contract to acquire supplies or services on the basis of direct labor hours at specified fixed hourly rates, including wages, overhead, general and administrative expenses, and profit and actual cost for materials.

The risk to contractors varies with the contract type. Under a cost-reimbursement contract, there is less risk to the contractor because the government will pay the contractor for expenses incurred. Under a fixed-price contract, the contractor bears most of the risk, since the contractor will be paid the same amount of money regardless of the cost of performance.

The type of contract used drives the application of certain FAR provisions.

3. What are the acquisition methods the government uses?

Full and Open Competition

In 1984, the Competition in Contracting Act (CICA) was enacted, requiring executive agencies to achieve "full and open competition" in the acquisition process unless an enumerated exception applies.

There are two basic methods of full and open competition:

- Sealed bidding
  - ◇ Under sealed bidding, the government issues an "Invitation for Bids" (IFB).
  - ◇ The government is required to rigidly adhere to formal procedures.
  - ◇ An agency must award the contract to the responsible bidder with the lowest responsive bid.
- Competitive negotiation
  - ◇ Under competitive negotiation procurement, the government issues a "Request for Proposals" (RFP).
  - ◇ Competitive negotiation utilizes more flexible procedures.
  - ◇ An agency may conduct discussions, evaluate offers, permit revisions, and award the contract using price and other factors.

4. Are there exceptions to "full and open competition"?

Federal Supply Schedule (FSS) Contracts

Under the General Services Administration (GSA) Schedules (also referred to as Multiple Award Schedules and Federal Supply Schedules) Program, the GSA establishes long-term government-wide contracts with commercial firms to provide access to millions of commercial supplies and services that can be ordered directly from GSA Schedule contractors or through the GSA Advantage! online shopping and ordering system.

Blanket Purchase Agreements (BPAs)

BPAs are a simplified method of filling anticipated repetitive needs for services and supplies. BPAs are like "charge accounts" established with GSA Schedule contractors by ordering agencies.

Government-Wide Acquisition Contracts (GWACs)

Four agencies have authority to host GWACs: the National Institutes of Health, the Environmental Protection Agency, the General Services Administration, and the National Aeronautics and Space Administration (NASA). GWACs are actually managed by the Office of Management and Budget Office of Federal Procurement Policy and are intended to provide information technology products and services. GWACs should not be confused with Multi-Agency Contracts (MACs), which individual agencies control and can permit other agencies to use.

5. What are multiple award contracts?

Historically, single award contracts (one contract, one contractor) were the norm. In 1994, the Federal Acquisition Streamlining Act (FASA) was passed, which made multiple award contracts a preference over single award contracts.

Multiple award contracts emphasize task orders:

- Individual contract orders are competed and awarded under overall contract vehicle.
- Competition for task orders is limited to multiple award contract companies.
- Contractors have limited rights to protest task order award. Contractors may only protest a task order award if the task order changes the maximum value, scope or period of the underlying contract, or if the task order is in excess of $10 million.

Summary

In order to begin to understand government contract formation, a company should understand that the FAR and agency supplements govern the acquisition process. Further, companies should note that the government typically uses cost-reimbursement, fixed-price, or incentive-based contracts, and, while ordinarily limited to utilizing competitive procurements (sealed bidding or competitive negotiation procurements), there are certain limited exceptions to "full and open competition" that the government may use.

Notes

Chapter 2

Top Things To Know About Government Contract Administration

Kevin T. Boyle, Vangent, Inc., J. Scott Hommer, III, and
Justin J. Wortman, Venable LLP

Once a contract has been formed, the other major aspect of federal government contracting is contract administration. There are several aspects of contract administration with the federal government that make it unlike working with any other party. This chapter provides an overview of these unique concepts.

1. Who may bind the federal government?

The Actual Authority Doctrine controls the administration of contracts with the federal government. This doctrine holds that only those officials given actual authority to administer a contract may bind the government. In other words, while a contractor may rely on the promises of a contracting officer who has been given actual authority to bind the government, a contractor may not rely on a contracting officer's technical representative, who has not been given actual authority to bind the government.

2. What rights to terminate a contract does the federal government have?

The federal government retains two methods for terminating a contract. These include:

- Termination for default: The termination for default is a sanction for nonperformance. The government may terminate a contract for a contractor's unexcused present or prospective failure to perform in accordance with the contract's terms, specifications, or delivery schedule.

◇ A termination for default renders a contractor liable for reprocurement costs and other damages.

◇ A contractor must also disclose any termination for default it has received within the last three years in all of its proposals.

- Termination for convenience: The government also retains a right to terminate a contract for convenience. This means that the government may terminate a contract in whole or in part at any time, when such a termination is in "the government's best interest." After a termination for convenience, a contractor is entitled to costs and profit through the date of termination.

3. What are contract flow-downs?

Many standard FAR contract clauses require the prime contractor to apply the terms of such clauses to its subcontractors. These provisions are called "flow-downs," and they bind the subcontractor just as they would a prime contractor. Prime contractors often go beyond mandatory flow-down clauses and impose additional or different terms and conditions on subcontractors, which often leads to issues for negotiation.

4. What right does the government have to change the requirements of a contract?

Unlike most commercial contracts, federal government contracts incorporate a FAR "changes clause." This clause allows the government to unilaterally issue orders to the contractor to change certain terms of the contract. When the government issues a change pursuant to the changes clause, a contractor may submit a request for equitable adjustment (REA) to the agreed-upon price, schedule and/or other applicable terms. When as a result of a change directed under the changes clause a contractor submits a REA to the agency contracting officer (CO), and the CO disapproves the REA in whole or in part, the contractor may decide to pursue the matter by submitting a certified claim under the Contract Disputes Act of 1978 (see Section VI, Chapter 4: Top Things To Know About Contract Disputes). Federal contracts for commercial items, which are governed by FAR Part 12, require bilateral modifications to change the terms of the contract.

5. What is the Christian Doctrine?

When the government contracting officer fails to include a mandatory contract clause—such as the termination for convenience clause—in a prime contract, the omitted clause will be "read into" and made applicable to the contract by operation of law under the so-called Christian Doctrine based on a federal appellate court decision. *See G.L. Christian & Assoc. v. United States*, 160 Ct. Cl. 1, 312 F.2d 418, *rehearing denied*, 160 Ct. Cl. 58, 320 F.2d 345, *cert. denied*, 375 U.S. 954 (1963).

6. How do commercial item acquisitions differ from a typical procurement?

To implement the federal government's preference for acquiring commercial items as established by the Federal Acquisition Streamlining Act of 1994, policies and procedures more closely resembling those of the commercial marketplace were added to the Federal regulations. For commercial item acquisitions, government contracting officers are authorized to tailor all but a few of the standard FAR contract clauses in a manner that is not inconsistent with customary commercial practice for the item being acquired.

Summary

Contracting with the federal government is unlike contracting with private parties. The government can only be bound by those who have been given actual authority to administer a contract and can unilaterally change a contract; and mandatory clauses can be "read into" contracts by operation of law even if a contracting officer fails to include the clauses in the contract.

Companies seeking to do business with the government should understand these differences in order to ensure that their rights are protected.

Notes

Chapter 3

Top Things To Know About Bid Protests

Kevin T. Boyle, Vangent, Inc., J. Scott Hommer, III, and
Justin J. Wortman, Venable LLP

If a contractor believes that the government has improperly drafted a solicitation or has inappropriately awarded a contract to another company, the contractor may choose to bring a bid protest. This chapter provides an overview of the types of protests and the bid protest process.

1.   What are the types of bid protests?

Pre-award protests
If there are improprieties in a solicitation, such as unduly restrictive specifications, a contractor may bring a pre-award protest challenging the ground rules to be applied by an agency in evaluating proposals.

Post-award protests
If the government is believed to have improperly awarded a contract to a company, another contractor may bring a post-award protest. Contractors participate in both sides of these types of protests.

- A company may challenge the government's awarding of a contract to a competitor (your company may protest the award).
- A company may intervene in the protest process to help defend the award of a contract against the protest of another company (your company is the intervenor).

2. What are the steps involved in litigating as the protestor?

1. The government announces the contract award.

2. A company requests a debriefing in writing: a debriefing must be requested in writing and within three days of receiving notice of the award to another company. In certain procurements, it is important to accept the first proposed debriefing date, since a stay of contract performance is calculated from this date.

3. The company receives the debriefing: The agency is required, at a minimum, to provide the following information:
   - The agency's evaluation of weak or deficient factors in the company's offer;
   - The overall evaluated cost and technical rating of the awardee's offer;
   - The overall evaluated cost and technical rating of your company's offer;
   - The overall ranking of the offers;
   - A summary of the rationale for the award; and
   - Reasonable responses to relevant questions posed by your company about the selection process.

4. A contractor decides whether to file a protest: There a number of factors to consider in deciding to bring a protest, including the likelihood of success in a protest and potential effects on the contractor's relationship with the agency.

5. The contractor decides where to file a protest: bid protests may be brought in different fora:
   - *The agency that awarded the contract:* This typically involves filing a protest letter with the agency contracting officer demonstrating grounds of protest and prejudice.
   - *The Government Accountability Office (the GAO):* This also requires filing a protest letter demonstrating grounds of protest and prejudice.
   - *U.S. Court of Federal Claims:* This requires filing a federal court "complaint" and a "motion for preliminary injunction" if seeking a stay of performance (a temporary restraining order).
   - *Office of Dispute Resolution for Acquisition (ODRA):* The Federal Aviation Administration maintains its own tribunal, the ODRA, to decide procurement disputes. Like the GAO, a filing at the ODRA typically involves filing a protest letter demonstrating grounds of protest and prejudice.

6. If the protest was timely filed, a protestor may be entitled to or otherwise may request a stay of contract performance, which stops the awardee from continuing performance of the contract. Protest timeliness rules are strictly enforced and must be scrupulously followed lest the contractor lose its right to protest and benefit from a stay of contract performance.

7. Protest procedures: Each forum has specific rules for filing and prosecuting a protest. These procedures include:
   1. Different timelines for filing particular documents;
   2. The extent of discovery that a protestor is allowed;
   3. Whether a protective order is issued to protect competition sensitive and source selection information; and
   4. Whether a stay of contract performance is issued during the pendency of the protest.

8. Contractor personnel (with the possible exception of in-house counsel in limited circumstances) are precluded from obtaining access to the agency's source selection documents and competitors' proposals during the protest. Such competition sensitive information is provided only to the contractor's legal counsel who satisfy certain requirements established by the forum deciding the protest.

9. Corrective action: The agency may sometimes take action prior to an official decision, remedying the violation of procurement law raised in the protest.

10. Protest decision: Once the appropriate decision-maker has considered the arguments on both sides, it will issue a decision about the allegations brought in the protest.

3. What if my company has been awarded a contract that another company protests?

If a company has been awarded a contract, the company may intervene in a protest to assist the agency in defending its actions against the protest. This can involve providing assistance to the agency, helping to shape the agency report, and attempting to narrow the scope of protest grounds.

An intervenor may participate in the protest process, by:

1. Engaging in discovery and assisting in the agency's opposition to the protester's discovery (e.g., document requests and requests to compel production of documents);
2. Reviewing the agency report or administrative record;
3. Participating in hearings;
4. Seeking the admission of experts under a protective order;
5. Preparing comments, motions and/or other briefs;
6. Handling supplemental grounds of protest/amendments to the Complaint; and/or

7. Controlling and/or avoiding settlement/corrective action.

An intervenor may also bring a request for summary dismissal, attempting to dismiss the protest on procedural grounds.

4. What potential remedies may a tribunal recommend?

The GAO bid protest regulations provide that the GAO may recommend that an agency implement any combination of the following remedies:

1. Refrain from exercising options under the contract;
2. Terminate the contract;
3. Recompete the contract;
4. Issue a new solicitation;
5. Award a contract consistent with statute and regulation; or
6. Such other recommendations as GAO determines necessary to promote compliance.

If GAO determines that a solicitation, proposed award, or award does not comply with statute or regulation, it may recommend that the contracting agency pay the protester the costs of:

1. Filing and pursuing the protest, including attorney's fees and consultant and expert witness fees; and
2. Bid and proposal preparation.

The U.S. Court of Federal Claims may order similar remedies to the GAO. The primary differences in the remedies issued by the two tribunal are as follows:

1. The Court of Federal Claims orders action by injunction, and the government is legally bound to follow the court's rulings. The GAO issues "recommendations," which the agency is not legally bound to—but virtually always does—follow.
2. Attorney's fees at the Court of Federal Claims are awarded pursuant to the Equal Access to Justice Act, 5 U.S.C. § 504; 28 U.S.C. § 2412.

An agency may provide remedies similar to those the GAO and United States Court of Federal Claims can recommend or order, respectively.

Summary

If a company believes that the government has improperly drafted a solicitation or awarded a contract, the company may bring a bid protest. In order to effectively assist counsel in the protest process, companies should understand the different tribunals in which protests may be brought and the unique procedures applicable to each forum.

GOVERNMENT ACCOUNTABILITY OFFICE PROTEST TIMELINE

ACTION	TIMELINE
Protest filed	If protesting a solicitation defect: No later than the date set for receipt of proposals.
	For post-award protests: No later than 10 calendar days after the basis of the protest is known or should have been known, except for procurements under which a debriefing is requested and, when requested, is required, in which case, the protester must wait until after the debriefing date offered to the protester.
	An automatic suspension of contract award is available (but subject to override) at the later of the following days: if a protest is filed within 10 days of contract award or if a written request for a debriefing is submitted, the protester accepts the first offered debriefing date, the protester files a protest within 5 calendar days of the debriefing and allows 1 day for the GAO to inform the agency.
GAO notifies agency of protest	Within 1 calendar day after protest is filed
Applications filed for access to GAO's protective order	Within 3 calendar days of receipt of the GAO's protective order
Request for hearing	No time specified
When the protester files a specific request for documents, the agency must provide the GAO and all parties with a list of the documents (or portions thereof) it intends to produce	At least 5 calendar days prior to filing the agency report

ACTION	TIMELINE
Objections to the scope of the agency's proposed production of documents due	Within 2 calendar days of receipt of the list
Agency report due	Within 30 calendar days after notification by the GAO of protest
Request for additional documents due	Within 2 calendar days after existence or relevance is known
Comments to the agency report due	Within 10 calendar days after receipt of the agency report
Post-hearing briefs due	Within 5 calendar days after the hearing or as notified
GAO decision due	Within 100 calendar days after the protest was filed
Request for reconsideration due	Within 10 calendar days after the basis of reconsideration is known or should have been known, whichever is earlier
Entitlement to costs	Within 15 calendar days of agency corrective action
Claim for costs	If the GAO recommends payment of costs, within 60 calendar days of the GAO's recommendation

Chapter 4

Top Things To Know About Contract Disputes

Kevin T. Boyle, Vangent, Inc., J. Scott Hommer, III, and
Justin J. Wortman, Venable LLP

During contract performance, if a contractor has a dispute with the government, this dispute must be resolved by following specific procedures. This chapter provides an overview of the contract dispute process.

1. What law governs contract disputes with the federal government?

The Contract Disputes Act of 1978 (CDA) governs contract disputes.

- The CDA codified a special process for disputes arising under a Government contract between the government and the contractor.
- Contractors must follow the mandated procedures of the CDA, or risk waiving or otherwise losing their right to proceed against the agency.
- The FAR implements the CDA through the standard "Disputes Clause."
  - ◇ The Disputes Clause defines a claim as: "A written demand or written assertion by one of the contracting parties seeking, as a matter of right, the payment of money in a sum certain, the adjustment or interpretation of contract terms, or other relief arising under or relating to [the] contract."
  - ◇ The Disputes Clause requires contractors to continue their performance pending resolution of a dispute with the government. Failure to continue performance may provide a basis for a default termination.

2.   How does a contractor present a claim?

A contractor initiates the dispute process by submitting a claim to the contracting officer. A proper claim:

1.   Must include a written demand;
2.   Must seek payment in a sum certain or other contract relief;
3.   Must be sought as a matter of right; and
4.   Must be certified by the contractor if over $100,000.

If the contractor and the contracting officer are unable to reach a resolution, the contracting officer must issue a final decision within 60 days or, if the claim is for more than $100,000, advise when the claim will be decided. If the contracting officer has not issued a final decision within 60 days, the contractor may proceed with its claim.

Once a final decision (or sufficient passage of time) has occurred, the contractor may appeal the decision to the cognizant Board of Contract Appeals or the U.S. Court of Federal Claims.

3.   What are the steps involved in litigating a claim?

1.   Submission of a claim and request that the contracting officer issue a final decision.
2.   Issuance of the contracting officer's final decision (or passage of sufficient time).
3.   Notice of appeal with the Civilian Agency Board of Contract Appeals or Armed Services Board of Contract Appeals or the U.S. Court of Federal Claims. Once a notice of appeal has been filed with one of the boards, the litigation follows the steps below:
     • The contractor files its complaint, alleging its claim.
     • The government files its answer, usually denying the grounds for the claim.
     • The contractor is provided the "Rule 4 File" (essentially, discovery of documents).
     • Additional discovery, if necessary, is taken.
     • The board conducts hearings, if necessary.
     • The board issues a decision.
4.   Appeal, if necessary, to the U.S. Court of Appeals for the Federal Circuit.

4.   What timelines apply to the submission of a claim?

1.   The statute of limitations for bringing a claim is 6 years.
2.   A claim may be denied as untimely, however, if:
     - The contract contained a notice provision requiring notice within a shorter period;
     - The government is prejudiced by the contractor's delay in the submission of its claim; or
     - If final payment has been made, it will usually bar claims based on alleged changes to the contract.

5.   How does a contractor prove its claim?

1.   A contractor bears the burden of proving entitlement and damages for its claims.
2.   In order to prove a claim, a contractor must be able to show:
     - Government conduct or inaction;
     - Directly caused an increase in the contractor's costs; and
     - The amount of increased costs; to prove its increased costs with "reasonable certainty" (which is the applicable standard), the contractor may provide:
       ▷   Actual costs;
       ▷   Reasonable estimates; or
       ▷   Expert testimony and reports.

6.   What if a subcontractor wishes to bring a claim against the government?

1.   Generally, if a subcontractor is an aggrieved party, the subcontractor may not bring a claim directly against the government because the subcontractor is not in privity of contract with the government.
2.   Instead, the prime contractor must bring a so-called "pass-through" claim on behalf of the subcontractor.
3.   Typically, a prime contractor may only bring a claim on behalf of a subcontractor if the prime contractor remains liable to the subcontractor, i.e., the prime contractor is required to pay the subcontractor.
4.   The prime contractor must certify the subcontractor's claim. The prime contractor certifies not that the claim is certain, but only that it believes the claim has good grounds.

Summary

Once a company begins performing a contract, if a dispute arises, it is important to know that the Contract Disputes Act governs, and that the company will be required to follow the specific procedures outlined above to ensure that the claim is presented and filed properly.

LITIGATION PATHWAYS FOR GOVERNMENT CONTRACT DISPUTES

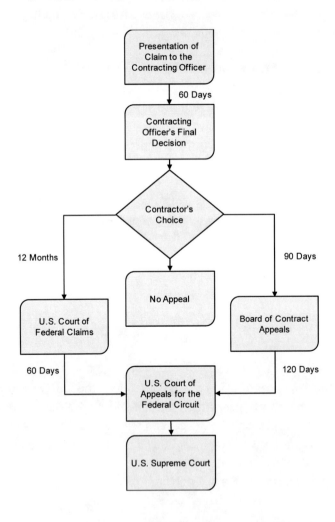

Chapter 5

Top Things To Know About Organizational Conflicts of Interest

Kevin T. Boyle, Vangent, Inc., J. Scott Hommer, III, and Justin J. Wortman, Venable LLP

The regulations governing federal government contracting seek to maintain adequate objectivity in the procurement process. This chapter provides an overview of organizational conflicts of interest, one of the important areas in the government's focus on ensuring objectivity.

1. What is an organizational conflict of interest (OCI)?

According to FAR 2.101, an OCI occurs when, because of activities or relationships with other persons, a person (defined to include an organization) is unable or potentially unable to render impartial assistance or advice to the government, or the person's objectivity in performing the contract work is or might otherwise be impaired, or a person has an unfair competitive advantage.

2. What regulations apply to OCIs?

OCIs are addressed in FAR Subpart 9.5, which indicates a concern with actual and potential conflicts and directs measures to be taken to detect and mitigate both.

FAR Subpart 9.5 requires the contracting officer to perform a number of tasks, directing the CO to:

1. Identify and evaluate potential OCIs as early as possible in the acquisition process;
2. Avoid, neutralize or mitigate significant potential OCIs before contract award;

3. Award the contract to the apparent successful offeror, unless the OCI cannot be avoided or mitigated; and
4. Request a waiver of the OCI if the contracting officer finds such a waiver is in the best interest of the government.

3. What are the types of OCIs?

There are three types of OCIs.

Unequal access to information

Unequal access to information OCIs arise where a firm has access to nonpublic information as part of its performance of a government contract and where that information may provide the firm a competitive advantage in a later competition for a government contract.

- A contractor may have an unfair competitive advantage if the contractor has possession of proprietary information of other firms or information obtained in performance of other government contracts not available to other competitors. Contractors should be aware that employing consultants that have had access to such source selection information may create an unequal access to information OCI.
- However, information obtained through performance as an incumbent is not deemed to be an unfair advantage in a recompetition for the same contract.

Biased ground rules

Biased ground rules OCIs occur where a firm, as part of its performance of a government contract, has in some sense set the ground rules for another government contract by, for example, writing the statement of work or the specifications.

- Contractors are disqualified from later source selections.
- Moreover, the GAO presumes in these cases that setting the ground rules gives the contractor an actual benefit and competitive advantage.

Impaired objectivity

Impaired objectivity OCIs occur where a firm's work under one government contract could entail evaluating itself or an affiliated entity, either through an assessment of performance under another contract or an evaluation of proposals.

In these "impaired objectivity" cases, the concern is that the firm's ability to render impartial advice to the government could appear to be undermined by its relationship with the entity whose work product is being evaluated. The conflict is caused by the very fact that the contractor is aware that its advice might have an impact on its company.

4. Why are OCIs a growing industry issue?

- Consolidation in the federal contracting sector—companies purchasing one another, consolidating the work performed under contracts.
- The government's increasing outsourcing of testing, evaluation, and analysis of systems and programs.
- Increasing reliance on performance-based contracting creates situations where a contractor can devise the means for contract performance that is beneficial to its industry segment.
- The increasing reliance on multiple award indefinite delivery/indefinite quantity (IDIQ) contracts limits the pool of contractors for particular tasks.
- Bid protests filed by contractors have increasingly alleged violation of the FAR OCI regulations as a ground of protest. Bid protests alleging OCI issues have experienced some success, particularly with the GAO.

5. How can OCIs be mitigated?

Unequal access to information
The GAO has found that an "unequal access to information" OCI may be mitigated by firewalling, and otherwise separating the individual or entity with the information from the rest of the company.

Biased ground rules
"Biased ground rules" OCIs are more difficult to mitigate. Typically, firewalling the conflicted entity is not enough to mitigate the OCI. Divesting the conflicted entity may adequately mitigate the conflict.

Impaired objectivity
It is difficult to mitigate an impaired objectivity OCI because it infects the entity, rather than individuals. Firewalls are typically not enough. Despite the difficulty, however, it is possible to mitigate impaired objectivity OCIs, often with firewalled subcontractors or other mitigation strategies, such as divestiture of the conflicted entities.

Summary

The federal government has become increasingly concerned with organizational conflicts of interest. Companies seeking to do business with the government should be aware of the three types of OCIs, unequal access to information OCIs, biased ground rules OCIs, and impaired objectivity OCIs, as well as the various potential strategies available to companies to mitigate these OCIs.

Chapter 6

Top Things To Know About Personal Conflicts of Interest

Kevin T. Boyle, Vangent, Inc., J. Scott Hommer, III, and
Justin J. Wortman, Venable LLP

In addition to the government's focus on organizational conflicts of interest, the government is also concerned with personal conflicts of interest. This chapter provides an overview of the recent developments in, and likely future direction of, personal conflicts of interest law.

1. What is a personal conflict of interest (PCI)?

The FAR does not currently provide a definition of a PCI. A proposed revision to the FAR, described more fully below, would define a PCI as "a situation in which a covered employee has a financial interest, personal activity, or relationship that could impair the employee's ability to act impartially and in the best interest of the government when performing under the contract." The Department of Defense (DOD) has described a PCI as "a situation where an individual is employed by [a federally funded research and development center] or a defense contractor company and is in a position to materially influence DOD's recommendations and/ or decisions and, because of his/her personal activities, relationships, or financial interests, may lack or appear to lack objectivity or appear to be unduly influenced by personal financial interest."

2. What laws apply to PCIs?

A number of statutory and regulatory provisions apply to government employees to address personal conflicts of interest.

- Title 18 of the U.S. Code addresses representational activities, post-government employment, financial interests, and payment for official actions.
- Other statutes limit outside employment, limit permissible gifts, and impose other restrictions.
- The Procurement Integrity Act 41 U.S.C. § 423 also imposes restrictions on employees involved in the award or administration of contracts.
- The Defense Federal Acquisition Regulation Supplement imposes certain ethics requirements on contractors.
- Contractors are subject to the requirements of the Sarbanes-Oxley Act of 2002.
- Executive Order 13490, signed by President Obama on January 21, 2009, requires political appointees in executive agencies to sign a pledge of conduct concerning, among other things, lobbying and accepting gifts.

3. How are the laws governing PCIs developing?

The Duncan Hunter National Defense Authorization Act for 2009 required the government to take a number of actions concerning PCIs, including:

1. Developing rules on personal services contracts;
2. Developing a personal conflicts of interest clause to include in solicitations;
3. Developing a government-wide policy on personal conflicts of interest by contractor employees performing work closely associated with inherently governmental activities; and
4. Determining whether FAR revisions are necessary to address personal conflicts of interest by contractor employees performing functions not closely associated with inherently governmental functions.

As a result, revisions to the FAR have been proposed.

1. If enacted, the revisions will require contractors to have procedures in place to:
   - Screen for potential PCIs;
   - Inform covered employees of their obligations with regard to PCIs;
   - Maintain effective oversight to verify compliance with PCI requirements;
   - Timely report any PCI violations to the contracting officer; and
   - Take appropriate disciplinary action with employees who fail to comply with PCI policies.

2. The FAR revisions also allow the head of the contracting activity, in exceptional circumstances, to agree to the mitigation of a personal conflict of interest or waive the requirement to prevent conflict of interest for a particular employee, if he or she determines in writing that such mitigation or waiver is in the best interest of the government.

3. The FAR revisions also allow the government certain remedies if a contractor is found to have violated the requirements, including suspension of contract payments, loss of award fee, termination for cause, and suspension or debarment.

Summary

In addition to organizational conflicts of interest, the government is also concerned with personal conflicts of interest, which may occur because of an employee's ability to influence the government or because an employee's interests create a conflict or the appearance of a conflict of interest. Future federal laws will almost certainly require companies to take additional efforts to deal with personal conflicts of interest, including, among other things, screening employees and reporting potential violations to the government.

Notes

Chapter 7

Top Things To Know About "Revolving Door" Issues

Kevin T. Boyle, Vangent, Inc., J. Scott Hommer, III, and
Justin J. Wortman, Venable LLP

Besides the government's focus on organizational and personal conflicts of interest, the federal government is also concerned with revolving door issues. This chapter summarizes restrictions placed upon government employees who leave government service to work in the private sector.

1. What is the "revolving door," and why is it an issue?

Federal statutes place post-employment restrictions on officers and employees of the government who move between the public and private sectors. Doing so can lead to concerns over impartiality and undue influence.

There are several substantive prohibitions, each varying in:

- The type of officer or employee affected;
- The duration of the restriction;
- The individual's involvement with the program in the federal government; and
- The scope of the restriction.

2. What restrictions are placed on "current" Executive Branch employees?

Officers and employees in the Executive Branch are generally prohibited from seeking future employment and working on official acts simultaneously if the official actions may be of significant benefit to the potential employer.

Under limited circumstances, however, the government may grant a waiver. These situations include:

- When the employee's self-interest is "not so substantial" as to affect the integrity of services provided by the employee.
- If the need for the employee's services outweighs the potential for a conflict of interest, according to Federal regulations.

3. What restrictions are placed on "former" Executive Branch employees?

A former Executive Branch employee is permanently banned from communicating or appearing on behalf of another person, with the intent to influence the government, in connection with a particular matter, if:

1. The United States or District of Columbia is a party or has a direct or substantial interest in the matter;
2. The matter involves a specific party or parties; and
3. The former employee participated "personally and substantially" as a Federal Government employee.
   - "Personally and substantially" means "active and significant involvement" in certain activities "directly related" to the particular matter in question.
   - Participating "personally" means participating "directly" and includes direct and active supervision of subordinates.
   - Participating "substantially" means that the official's involvement is "of significance to the matter," i.e., more than perfunctory or on an administrative or peripheral issue.

The goal of this lifetime restriction is to prevent a former government employee who has participated in a matter while employed by the government from switching sides and later representing another person on the same matter before the United States.

A former Executive Branch employee may, however, work "behind the scenes." For example, a former Executive Branch employee may advise a contractor on preparing a proposal for a government procurement managed by the government entity that previously employed the Executive Branch employee, provided that the Executive Branch employee did not participate personally and substantially as a federal government employee with respect to the particular matter and was not a procurement official as described in item 6 below.

4. What other restrictions are placed upon "former" Executive Branch officials?

For 2 years after an employee leaves government service, a former Executive Branch employee is prohibited from communicating or appearing with the intent to influence a particular matter, on behalf of anyone other than the government, when:

1. The government is a party or has a direct interest in the matter;
2. The former employee knew or should have known that the matter was pending under his/her official responsibility during a period of one year prior to leaving government service; and
3. At the time of the employee's participation in the particular matter, specific parties other than the government were involved.

This restriction prohibits communication with, or appearance before, a former agency, on behalf of another with intent to influence, on any matter where official action is sought.

It prohibits direct lobbying contacts with former colleagues or with any political appointee in the Executive Branch.

Behind-the-scenes assistance is permitted.

Other communications to other agencies (except political appointees) are permitted.

5. What is the "cooling-off" period for senior Executive Branch officials?

For one year after a senior Executive Branch employee leaves government service, the former senior government employee is prohibited from communicating or appearing before any officer or employee of the department or agency in which the former employee served in connection with **any matter** where the former employee is:

1. Appearing on behalf of another person;
2. Intending to influence the government; and

3. Seeking official action by any officer or employee of the department or agency where the former employee worked.

This one-year cooling-off period applies only to senior government officials (such as officers at pay grade O-7 and above, and those employees on the Executive Schedule).

6. What restrictions are placed upon former procurement officials?

A former government employee may not accept compensation from a contractor for 1 year after the employee:

1. Served as the procuring contracting officer, the source selection authority, a member of the source selection board, or as the chief of the technical or financial evaluation team in which the contractor was awarded a contract greater than $10 million; or
2. Served as the program manager, deputy program manager, or administrative contracting officer for a contract awarded to the contractor in excess of $10 million; or
3. Personally made certain decisions regarding a contract held by the contractor in excess of $10 million. These decisions include:

   - The decision to award a contract, subcontract, modification of a contract or subcontract, or a task order or delivery order in excess of $10,000,000;
   - A decision to establish overhead or other rates applicable to a contract valued in excess of $10,000,000;
   - A decision to approve issuance of a contract payment or payments in excess of $10,000,000; or
   - A decision to pay or settle a claim in excess of $10,000,000.

7. What steps should contractors who are contemplating hiring an Executive Branch employee take?

Contractors that contemplate hiring an Executive Branch employee should request the federal employee to provide the contractor a copy of the designated agency ethics official's advisory opinion describing the post-employment restrictions to which the federal employee is subject. Contractors should review the agency ethics advisory opinion in conjunction with performing its own independent analysis prior to extending an offer of employment.

Summary

Congress has passed restrictions on the types of work executive branch, senior executive branch, and procurement officials may engage in immediately after employment with the government. In order to avoid potential problems, companies should understand the myriad restrictions placed on current and former government employees, as well as ways to ensure that the company's interests are protected, including securing ethics advisory opinions and performing independent own analyses prior to extending an offer of employment.

Notes

Chapter 8

Top Things To Know About Ethics and Business Practices

Kevin T. Boyle, Vangent, Inc., J. Scott Hommer, III, and Justin J. Wortman, Venable LLP

Federal statutes and regulations prescribe a number of policies and procedures requiring contractors to avoid improper business practices and conflicts of interest. Two examples of improper business practices, gratuities and subcontractor kickbacks, are discussed below, as well as an overview of laws regarding giving and receiving gifts.

1. What are the prohibitions on gratuities?

18 U.S.C. § 201(1)(a) prohibits anyone from:

1. Directly or indirectly giving, offering, or promising,
2. Anything of value,
3. To any official,
4. "For or because of any official act performed or to be performed."

FAR 3.101-2 and 52.203-3 prohibit offering or giving a gratuity to any government officer, official or employee when the gratuity is intended to influence an award or result in favorable treatment.

Violations may result in a fine or imprisonment for up to two years, or both.

2. What are the prohibitions on kickbacks?

The Anti-Kickback Act of 1986 (codified at FAR 3.502, 52.203-7) was passed primarily to deter subcontractors or vendors from making payments to a prime contractor, and prime contractors from accepting payments, for the purpose of improperly obtaining or rewarding favorable treatment in connection with a prime contract or subcontract.

The Anti-Kickback Act also prohibits payment of kickbacks to government employees.

The act defines the term kickback broadly, to include: "any money, fee, commission, credit, gift, gratuity, thing of value, or compensation of any kind which is provided directly or indirectly, to any prime contractor, prime contractor employee, subcontractor, or subcontractor employee for the purpose of improperly obtaining or rewarding favorable treatment in connection with a prime contract or in connection with a subcontract relating to a prime contract."

3. What are the prohibitions on providing or receiving gifts?

A gift is defined as any "gratuity, favor, discount, entertainment, hospitality, forbearance, or other item having monetary value."

The general rule to avoid improper appearance with gifts is to never request or ask for gifts, entertainment or any other business courtesies from people doing business with your company.

Furthermore, a contractor should never provide a gift or entertainment that the contractor is aware violates another entity's gift and entertainment policy.

If a contractor is offered or intends to provide gifts, it should not provide or accept from an outside business partner, whether actual or potential, any gift with a market value in excess of $250. This limit applies provided the gift:

1. Is not for any improper purpose;
2. Does not violate law or regulation;
3. Is infrequent; and
4. Does not violate the giving company's general gift rules.

Most contractors follow the government guidelines in treating gifts the same way.

4. What are the restrictions on providing gifts to employees of the government?

The general rule is that a contractor should not provide any gifts to an employee of the government. See, e.g., FAR 3.101-1 ("The general rule is to avoid strictly any conflict of interest or even the appearance of a conflict of interest in Government-contractor relationships.")

Exceptions to the general rule include:

1. A contractor may provide gifts of $20 or less, subject to the following.
   - The gift must be $20 or less per source per occasion.
   - This exception does not apply to gifts of cash or of investment interests such as stock, bonds, or certificates of deposit.
   - A government employee may not receive gifts exceeding $50 from a single source in a single year.
   - If a government employee is offered a gift worth more than $20 on any occasion, the government employee may not pay for the value exceeding $20 to make the net value of the gift less than $20.
2. A contractor providing gifts based on personal relationships. In order for this exception to apply, the circumstances must be clear that the gift is motivated by a family relationship or personal relationship rather than the position of the employee.
3. A company providing discounts and similar benefits.
   - This exception includes reduced memberships or fees for participation in professional organization activities offered to all government employees.
   - This exception also includes opportunities and benefits, including favorable rates and commercial discounts offered to members of a group or class in which membership is unrelated to government employment.
4. A company offering awards and honorary degrees of less than $200 in value (including meals and entertainment at awards presentation).
5. A company providing gifts of free attendance at widely-attended gatherings provided that the agency determines that attendance is in its interest.
6. A company providing gifts that are the result of the employment of an employee's spouse or the employee's own outside business activities, when those activities are not connected to the employee's official position.
7. A company providing modest refreshments (e.g., coffee and donuts) when not served as a meal. Conversely, most any meal (even a sandwich) is not permitted even if the value of the meal is less than $20.

8. A company giving greeting cards and items with little intrinsic value, such as a plaque or certificate.
9. A contractor providing prizes in contests open to the public.
10. The company providing anything for which the government employee pays market value (i.e., face value).

Summary

Federal law prohibits contractors from engaging in a number of improper business practices and creating conflicts of interest. In order to avoid potential problems, contractors should understand the prohibitions on gratuities and subcontractor kickbacks, as well as the laws governing giving and receiving gifts.

Chapter 9

Top Things To Know About Government Remedies for Contractor Wrongdoing

Kevin T. Boyle, Vangent, Inc., J. Scott Hommer, III, and
Justin J. Wortman, Venable LLP

The government possesses a range of contractual remedies it may use to counter contractor wrongdoing, including voiding and rescinding contracts and imposing monetary penalties. In addition, other statutory and regulatory remedies are available to the government. Two of the more typical remedies that are employed arise from the False Claims Act and suspension and debarment.

This chapter provides an overview of these remedies.

1. What is the False Claims Act?

The False Claims Act states that a contractor is subject to criminal liability, 18 U.S.C. § 287, and civil liability, 31 U.S.C. § 3729, if it submits false or fraudulent claims for payment to the government.

Criminal remedies include:

1. Prison sentences of up to 5 years; and
2. Criminal fines of up to $250,000.

Civil remedies include

1. Treble damages; and
2. Fines per invoice/occurrence of $5,000 to $10,000.

In addition to actions brought directly by the government, the act authorizes *qui tam* relators ("whistleblowers") to sue contractors in the name of the government, and to receive a significant portion of the monetary remedies if successful.

Common examples of False Claims Act liability include:

1. Cost or labor mischarging, i.e., misapplying charges to contracts that have not run out.
2. Overcharging for products provided to the government

2. What is meant by suspension?

Suspension—and debarment, described in Section 3 below—are prospective remedies that the government employs to designate a contractor as ineligible to compete for future contracts.

A suspension action will be taken by an agency to disqualify a contractor temporarily from government contracting and government-approved subcontracting.

Suspensions can arise from numerous improper activities, including:

1. Fraud or a criminal charge arising in obtaining or performing a public contract;
2. Violating antitrust statutes related to submission of offers;
3. Embezzlement, theft, forgery, bribery, falsification or destruction of records;
4. Offenses indicating lack of business integrity or honesty;
5. Drug-Free Workplace Act violation;
6. Falsely affixing "Made in America" inscription;
7. Committing an unfair trade practice; and
8. Knowing failure by a "principal" to timely disclose to the government the following in connection with the award, performance, or closeout of a covered government contract:
   - Criminal law violations involving fraud, conflict of interest, bribery, or gratuities.
   - Civil False Claims Act violations (including employee retaliation claims).
   - Significant overpayments, other than overpayments resulting from contract financing payments as defined by FAR 32.001.

3.   What is meant by debarment?

Debarment is an action undertaken by an agency's debarment official to remove a contractor from government contracting and subcontracting for a specified period of time, usually no more than 3 years.

Along with the above-mentioned bases for suspension, debarment may be based on a violation of the terms of a government contract so serious as to justify debarment, such as:

1.   Willful failure to perform in accordance with the terms of one or more contracts; or
2.   A history of failure to perform, or of unsatisfactory performance of, one or more contracts.

A debarment precludes a contractor from contracting with any federal agency, unless the other agency provides a compelling reason for a waiver.

4.   What are the procedures for suspensions and debarments?

Except where an indictment or conviction for a criminal offense is the underlying offense, the due process surrounding the imposition of a debarment or suspension generally includes the provision of notice to the contractor (and any affiliates involved).

Generally, the contractor is permitted to submit an argument and, at least where there are material issues in dispute, present witnesses and evidence, prior to the imposition of a debarment or suspension.

Typically, an affiliate (e.g., parent company) is not subjected to debarment or suspension merely because it is the affiliate of an entity which is subject to debarment or suspension. The FAR does not exclude the possibility that the basis for suspension or debarment could be imputed to an affiliate company, however.

If imposed, a suspension generally lasts until a decision is issued with regard to debarment.

If a contractor receives notice of a proposed suspension, the contractor should seek advice of counsel as soon as possible.

Summary

Federal law provides the government with a number of contractual remedies it may use to punish contractor misconduct. These remedies include voiding and rescinding contracts and imposing monetary penalties. The government may also utilize statutory and regulatory remedies, such as suspension and debarment and those outlined in the False Claims Act. Companies seeking to do business with the government should understand the basics of these legal measures and take steps to ensure compliance.

Chapter 10

Top Things To Know About Ethics Compliance Programs

Kevin T. Boyle, Vangent, Inc., J. Scott Hommer, III, and
Justin J. Wortman, Venable LLP

The government has shown increased interest recently in ensuring that it contracts only with companies that uphold high ethical standards. To that end, the government has promulgated new regulations obligating contractors to incorporate new ethics requirements as part of their business practices. This chapter provides an overview of those requirements and how companies can begin to meet them.

1. What sort of ethics requirements does the FAR incorporate?

Prior to December 2007, the FAR did not contain a specific requirement for contractors to have a formal code of ethics or business conduct program. Two changes have been made to the FAR since December 2007 regarding a code of ethics and business conduct program.

First FAR change—December 2007

The first change requires contractors and subcontractors receiving awards of contracts expected to exceed $5 million (including options) and with a performance period of 120 days or more to:

1. Have a written code of business ethics and conduct within 30 days of award;
2. Implement a formal awareness or training program on the code within 90 days of award;
3. Develop internal controls to support the code, also within 90 days of award; and
4. Display a hotline poster that provides telephone numbers to report misconduct.

Second FAR change—December 12, 2008

The second change requires contractors meeting different requirements to:

1. Have a written code of business ethics and conduct;
2. Make the code available to all employees involved in performance of the contract, including prime contractor employees, subcontractors, and vendors;
3. Exercise due diligence to prevent and detect improper conduct;
4. Promote an organizational culture that encourages ethical conduct and a commitment to compliance with the law;
5. Timely disclose, in writing, to the agency Office of Inspector General, with a copy to the contracting officer, whenever, in connection with the award, performance, or closeout of any government contract or subcontract, the contractor has credible evidence of a violation of federal criminal law involving fraud, conflict of interest, bribery or gratuity violations found in Title 18 of the U.S. Code; or a violation of the civil False Claims Act.
6. Fully cooperate in government audits, investigations, or corrective actions relating to contract fraud and corruption.

2. What should be in an ethics program?

The new FAR ethics requirements provide some guidance for what should be in an ethics program. According to FAR 52.203-13, a reliable program will include:

- Assignment of high-level responsibility within the company for the ethics program;
- Adequate review of company business practices;
- Ethics reporting hotlines;
- Instructing employees on how to use hotlines;
- Internal and external audits; and
- Disciplinary action for improper action.

3. How should contractors go about implementing the FAR requirements?

There are five guiding principles for implementing the new FAR requirements:

1. Tone: The concept of *tone at the top* means that an ethics-based culture is best set—and must be set—at the highest levels of the organization.

2. *Inclusiveness*: Ethics programs must set the tone for compliance by involving everyone in the organization.

3. *Thoroughness*: A company's ethics program must not only fulfill the requirements of the new FAR provisions, but must do so thoroughly, i.e., the program must be both broad and deep.

4. *Transparency*: Good training programs must have established processes in place that avoid even the appearance of favoritism or OCIs, and provide employees the chance to review and ask questions about training and violations reporting processes.

5. *Follow-through*: If a violation occurs that warrants disciplinary action, that action must be taken without delay.

4. What are some tips for compliance programs?

- Provide the option of online training, since online training is often most convenient.
- Set aside a specific time and place for training. Setting aside a particular time ensures that all employees can fit the training in during working hours.
- Send out periodic ethics e-mail updates or advisories. Even if most employees delete them, they are reminded of the importance of ethics in the organization.
- Bring in outside counsel to review ethics policies and training handouts. A fresh set of eyes should ensure that company policy is in line with government expectations and industry practice.
- Give employees repeated opportunities to ask questions. Make sure that employees are regularly able to ask questions and to do so in a variety of ways (in person, by e-mail, over the phone, submission to an anonymous drop box, etc.).
- Acknowledging ethical behavior. Acting ethically can, and should, be rewarded just as employees are awarded for business development, productivity, and other actions that benefit the company.
- Make sure new employees are promptly given policies, training, and other resources. New employees often fall through the cracks and must wait until the next training cycle, which may occur well after they have worked on procurements in which their knowledge of the rules is essential for full compliance.

Summary

In recent years, the federal government has become increasingly focused on ethics requirements. In order to ensure compliance with these news laws, companies should review their ethics compliance programs to ensure that they are robust enough to meet the legal requirements.

Chapter 11

Top Things To Know About Intellectual Property Rights in Government Contracts

Kevin T. Boyle, Vangent, Inc., J. Scott Hommer, III, and
Justin J. Wortman, Venable LLP

The FAR and Agency Supplements to the FAR contain complex provisions applicable to intellectual property rights. These rights can be broken down into two major categories of intellectual property: patents and technical data. This chapter provides an overview of the government's treatment of both.

1. What patent rights do contractors retain in government contracts?

The FAR includes two different clauses that may be included in contracts or subcontracts for "experimental, developmental, or research work" and that allow either the contractor or the government to retain patent rights to inventions made in the performance of a contract.

Generally, the contractor may retain title to the patent.

1. Under this clause, a contractor may, after following specific steps to disclose the invention, elect to retain title to the invention. The government retains the right to modify the contractor's title in certain limited circumstances.
2. The government is granted a license to the patent.
    *   The government retains a "nonexclusive, nontransferable, irrevocable, paid-up license to practice or have practiced for or on behalf of the United States the subject invention throughout the world."
    *   This license allows the government the right to have other companies produce the patented item for sale to the government.

3. If the contractor elects not to retain title to the invention or fails to follow the proper procedures to retain title, the government may take over title.

In certain limited circumstances, the government may retain title to subject inventions.

1. If the contractor follows the appropriate disclosure procedures, the contractor is granted a revocable, non-exclusive, paid-up license.
2. The contractor, or an employee-inventor after consultation with the contractor, may request greater rights than the non-exclusive license ordinarily provided to the contractor.

2. What steps can a company take to ensure that it protects pre-existing patent rights?

A contractor can take a number of steps to ensure that patents created through private expense remain the property of the company, including:

1. Where reasonable and logical to do so, keep requirements for development out of a contract's scope of work;
2. In proposals for contracts, identify patents that the company already holds and which it intends to utilize in the performance of the contract;
3. Execute an agreement with the government prior to contract performance regarding the treatment of research and development costs and patents; and
4. Ensure that contracts do not include payments that could be construed as giving the government rights in pre-existing patents.

3. What rights to technical data do contractors retain under the FAR?

The FAR recognizes standard types of rights that the government may retain in technical data, which FAR 27.401 defines as "data other than computer software, which are of a scientific or technical nature." Technical data may include, for examples, specifications for hardware or information concerning proprietary processes. The rights recognized by the FAR include:

- *Unlimited rights*: When the government retains unlimited rights, the government requires a company to release the data to the government, and the government has the right to use, reveal, or reproduce the data as it deems appropriate. The government's rights include the ability to provide the data to other contractors for use in the performance of other government contracts.

- *Limited rights*: When the government retains limited rights, it typically requires a company to deliver technical data to it, but the data may be submitted under protective legend and the government agrees to keep the data confidential. The government may challenge the validity of a contractor's protective legend.

- *No rights*: When the government has no rights to technical data, a company is not required to deliver the data, and the government makes no claims to it.

- *Negotiated rights*: In addition to the three standard types of data rights that the government may retain, a contracting officer may also choose to negotiate a hybrid level of data rights for any given procurement. Similarly, agencies have developed slightly different types of data rights in their respective FAR supplements.

- *Restricted rights software*: When computer software is developed at private expense, the developer may submit the software to the government with restricted rights. The government may only copy restricted rights software to back-up the software, to perform software maintenance, to use with the original computer(s), or to switch to a back-up or replacement computer(s). Restricted rights software may not be disclosed outside the government for competitive purposes.

4. What rights to technical data do contractors retain under the DFARS?

Because the Department of Defense often purchases military-specific items that have no commercial counterparts, the DOD has developed its own set of data rights with its own particular procedures. These types of data rights include:

- *Unlimited rights*: When data are created using exclusively government funds (often through a research and development contract where the data is listed as a deliverable), the government retains unlimited rights to the data. When the government has unlimited rights to data, it retains the right to use, reproduce or reveal the data, including to a company's competitors.

- *Limited rights*: When data are created using exclusively private funds and are properly marked with a protective legend, the government may retain limited rights to it. In this case, while the company agrees to deliver the data to the government, the government must hold it in confidence. To protect limited rights data, a company must identify the data in its proposal and mark the data with a protective legend, containing particular information, when delivered. As under the FAR, the government may challenge the validity of a contractor's protective legend.

- *Government purpose license rights*: When data are developed using a combination of government and private funds, the government may negotiate government purpose license rights with the contractor. This type of data rights allows the government to reveal the data to another company to develop a second source of a product for the government (but not in the commercial market). To protect government purpose license rights data, a contractor must identify the data in its proposal, and the government will then negotiate the use of the data.

5. Why is marking technical data properly important?

When a contractor intends to retain rights to technical data, i.e., when the contractor intends to grant the government limited rights or government purpose license rights, it is imperative that the contractor either properly label the data with a protective legend or label the data for negotiation, respectively. Failure to do so may result in granting the government unlimited rights to the data, because such data is presumed to have been given with unlimited rights.

Summary

Federal law contains complicated requirements regarding intellectual property rights granted under government contracts. Companies seeking to do business with the federal government should understand that the government may be given different rights to technical data depending upon how the data are derived, how the creation of the data is funded, and whether the contractor marks the data with an appropriate legend. Contractors should also understand that federal law provides companies with different rights to patents, though the government will generally, at a minimum, retain a license to any patent created under a government contract.

ഐ ഐ ഐ

Chapter 12

Top Things To Know About Supporting the U.S. Government Overseas

Kevin T. Boyle, Vangent, Inc., J. Scott Hommer, III, and Justin J. Wortman, Venable LLP

Companies working with the federal government overseas may be subject to certain requirements not necessarily applicable to contractors working in the United States. These additional requirements include the Defense Base Act (DBA) and Status of Forces Agreements (SOFAs) that the federal government has entered into with other nations. This chapter provides an overview of these requirements.

1. What does the Defense Base Act require?

The DBA requires contractors and subcontractors to secure workers' compensation for employees working overseas. It accomplishes this by extending the Longshore and Harbor Workers' Compensation Act to cover the injury or death of employees working in a number of situations, including:

1. Outside the United States for private contractors at any military, air or naval base or on any land used by the United States for military or naval purposes;
2. Outside the continental United States on any public works government contract or subcontract;
3. On contracts performed outside the United States for contracts or subcontracts approved and funded under the Foreign Assistance Act; or
4. Outside the United States for contractors or subcontractors that provide welfare or similar services for the benefit of the armed forces.

Employees who meet these requirements are covered by the DBA, regardless of nationality.

The DBA provides medical, disability and death benefits to covered employees injured or killed during the course of employment, regardless of whether the injury or death occurred during normal working hours.

2. Are there exceptions to the DBA's coverage?

There are a number of exceptions to the DBA's coverage. These exceptions apply to classes of employees. Injuries or death to the following types of employees are not covered by the DBA:

- An employee subject to the provisions of the Federal Employees' Compensation Act;
- An employee engaged in agriculture, domestic service, or any employment that is casual and not in the usual course of the trade, business, or profession of the employer; and
- A master or member of a crew of any vessel.

3. What are the ramifications of not securing coverage as required by the DBA?

If a contractor fails to secure appropriate insurance, or self-insure, for the required DBA benefits, there are certain remedial actions the government may take, including:

- Requiring the company to secure the payment of the benefits.
  - ◇ A prime contractor may be liable for its subcontractor's benefits if the subcontractor fails to secure payment of the DBA benefits to its employee.
- Prosecuting the contractor or subcontractor.
  - ◇ The contractor may be convicted of a misdemeanor punishable by a fine not exceeding $10,000, or imprisonment not exceeding 1 year, or both.
  - ◇ If the contractor or subcontractor is a corporation, the president, secretary, and treasurer may be jointly and severally liable for the fine and/or imprisonment.

4. What are Status of Forces Agreements (SOFAs)?

The U.S. government frequently enters into agreements with foreign countries regarding the requirements and treatment of U.S. military personnel while in a foreign country. Although there are no formal requirements for SOFAs, these documents often include requirements that pertain to contractor personnel who are operating within the foreign country as well. There are several common areas in which SOFAs govern contractors. These include:

- *Business licensing/registration*: SOFAs will frequently spell out exactly what type of licensing and/or registration a contractor is required to obtain within a foreign nation.
- *Taxes*: SOFAs also frequently detail what foreign taxes are applicable to a contractor.
- *Criminal and civil jurisdiction*: SOFAs often provide a framework for whether the host nation will have criminal and/or civil jurisdiction over contractors and their personnel.
- *Registration*: SOFAs can contain requirements for the registration of vehicles and/or weapons used by contractors.
- *Employee exemptions*: SOFAs may provide details regarding exemptions for contractor personnel from the host nation:
  - ◇ Taxes;
  - ◇ Customs/importation fees; and/or
  - ◇ Labor laws.

Summary

Companies that perform work for the government overseas may be subject to requirements that are not necessarily applicable to companies working in the United States. In order to ensure that their rights are appropriately protected, companies should understand the Defense Base Act and any Status of Forces Agreements the U.S. government has entered into with the host nation.

Notes

SECTION VII
EMPLOYMENT LAW ISSUES

CONTENTS

Chapter 1

Guidelines on Interview Questions

Jacqueline R. Depew, Axiom

Interviewing applicants is an important step in ensuring that a company hires qualified individuals who will be successful and contribute to its business. Hiring managers and others who interview potential employees, or current employees who seek other positions, must also ensure that the interviews are conducted in a completely lawful manner.

Federal, state, and local laws impact the types of questions that may be asked during an interview. For example, the Civil Rights Act of 1964, as amended, prohibits discrimination on the basis of race, sex, color, national original and religion. The Age Discrimination in Employment Act prohibits discrimination against individuals based on their age (40 or above), the Americans with Disabilities Act of 1990, as amended, protects individuals with disabilities, and the recently enacted Genetic Information Nondiscrimination Act of 2008 prohibits discrimination against employees based on genetic information. Laws in Virginia, Maryland and the District of Columbia additionally protect individuals from discrimination based on marital status, and laws in the District of Columbia and Maryland prohibit discrimination against individuals based on sexual orientation, and based upon age for anyone over the age of 18 (in the District of Columbia) and of any age (in Maryland).

These are only examples of the numerous federal, state and local laws that prohibit discrimination based upon a myriad of factors. As a general rule, potential employers should only ask questions that are relevant to the hiring decision—that is, questions that are designed to elicit information that is relevant to the duties of the position for which the individual is being considered.

Inquiries related to age

Do Not Ask:	What is your date of birth?
	What is your age?
	When did you graduate from high school/college?
You May Ask:	Are you over the age of 18?

Inquiries related to gender, marital status and sexual orientation

Do Not Ask:	Are you married or engaged?
	Do you prefer to be called Ms., Miss or Mrs.?
	What is your maiden name?
	Do you have children?
	What are your childcare arrangements?
	Are you pregnant or planning to become pregnant?
You May Ask:	Are you able to work the following hours?
	Are you available to work overtime? (if overtime is expected or required, and if you ask it of both male and female candidates)
	Are you able to travel? (if travel is expected or required, and if you ask it of both male and female candidates)

Inquiries related to religion

Do Not Ask:	What religion are you?
	What church do you belong to?
	What clubs or organizations do you belong to?

Inquiries related to national origin or citizenship

Do Not Ask:	Where were you (or your parents) born?
	Are you a U.S. citizen? (unless citizenship is a job requirement, generally for purposes of a obtaining a security clearance)
	What is your native language?
You May Ask:	Are you legally eligible for employment in the United States?

Inquiries related to medical conditions and disabilities

Do Not Ask:	Do you have any mental or physical impairments or limitations?
	Do you have any disability or medical condition that will prevent you from performing the job?
	How did you become disabled? (even when disability is apparent)
	Do you use any medication?
	Have you ever filed a workers' compensation claim?
	How is your health?
	Have you ever been treated for a drug or alcohol problem?
You May Ask:	Would you be able to perform the essential functions of the job (after you describe what those essential functions are), either with or without an accommodation?
	How much time off did you take in your previous job? (But you cannot ask why).
	Did you receive any discipline in your previous job(s)?

Inquiries related to arrests and convictions

Do Not Ask:	Have you ever been arrested?
	Have you ever had a criminal charge expunged?
You May Ask:	Have you ever been convicted of a crime? If so, when, where and what was the conviction for? (You should inform the candidate that conviction of a crime would not necessarily disqualify him or her from consideration.)

Inquiries related to economic status

Do Not Ask:	Where do you live?
	Do you own your home?
	Have you ever declared bankruptcy?
	Have your wages ever been garnished?

While many of the questions detailed above are not per se unlawful, they can be used as evidence of discrimination. Following these guidelines, and asking only job-related questions during an interview will help avoid legal pitfalls.

Chapter 2

Investigating Sexual Harassment and Discrimination Complaints

Jacqueline R. Depew, Axiom

Responding promptly and appropriately to an employee's internal claim of sexual harassment or other type of harassment or discrimination, and conducting a thorough, impartial and timely investigation is critical to maintaining a productive, open, and harmonious work environment and minimizing legal risks. Accordingly, when conducting an investigation of an internal complaint, the following guidelines should be observed.

If an employee reports to you allegations of sexual harassment or other discrimination take it seriously and make yourself available immediately, if at all possible. Sit down with the employee in a private location and listen to what the employee has to say. Let the employee give his/her account of the situation first before you start asking questions, then ask follow-up questions to clarify any points and obtain as many details as possible. Take careful, detailed notes of everything the complainant says initially, and of the follow-up questions. *Do not* include your opinion, comments, thoughts, or conclusions in your notes, and do not share your thoughts or opinions with the complaining witness. At the conclusion of the interview, ask the complainant what resolution he/she is looking for, to help gauge how seriously the complainant takes the allegations, and how difficult or easy the resolution might be. Keep in mind, however, that the complainant's proposed resolution may not be appropriate—either because it is too harsh, too lenient, unreasonable, or otherwise inappropriate.

At the conclusion of the interview, explain that the company takes the allegations seriously and will conduct a prompt and thorough investigation and will take appropriate action based on the results of the investigation. Remind the employee that there will be no retaliation for making a complaint and that if any additional inappropriate activity occurs, the employee should report it to you. *Do not* promise confidentiality. Explain that you will keep the information as confidential as possible, but that information will be shared with those who have a need to know as part of the investigation. Tell the employee that you *prefer* that he/she not discuss the investigation with other employees or anyone outside the company. (Keep in mind that you cannot prohibit any employee from reporting their claim to the Equal Employment Opportunity Commission or similar administrative agency, or from filing a lawsuit.) Be aware that once the employee makes allegations of harassment or discrimination, the company is obligated to conduct an investigation, even if the complainant asks you not to.

After receiving a complaint, *do not* immediately approach the alleged wrongdoer and report the complaint and ask if there is anything to it. You need to come up with a plan before you start talking with those involved or potentially involved. However, depending on the nature and seriousness of the allegations, it may be necessary to separate the complaining employee from the alleged harasser promptly. This can be a very difficult decision, and must be made very carefully, and ideally should be made with input from your general counsel and/or outside counsel. You should not automatically send the complaining employee home or move him/her to another department, area, or location—unnecessarily or unfairly burdening the complainant could be viewed as retaliation.

Preparing for the investigation

Upon receipt of the complaint, determine the necessary scope of the investigation based on whether the alleged actions are minor or significant. If additional investigation is necessary, you must decide who needs to be involved—who should conduct the investigation, who should be notified of the claim, and who should be interviewed.

Selecting an investigator
In order to avoid questions of impartiality, it is best to use an investigator outside of the reporting lines of the alleged wrongdoer. If the alleged wrongdoer is the president or CEO of the company, using an outside investigator is highly recommended. The investigator should be directed to conduct the investigation, prepare a report of his or her factual findings and leave it to the appropriate officials within the company, or the company's board of directors, if appropriate, to determine appropriate action based on the findings.

Notifying company officials
Shortly after receiving the complaint, the appropriate company officials must decide whether others in the company, such as the alleged wrongdoer's supervisor, need to be notified. If the allegations are against a senior executive other than the president or CEO, it may be appropriate to notify the president and/or CEO of the allegations and keep him/her apprised of the investigation. If the allegation is against the president or CEO, the company officials should consider whether it is necessary or appropriate to notify the company's board of directors (or a subset thereof).

Identifying potential witnesses
If the complaining employee identified individuals who may have relevant information concerning the claim, you will need to determine which of them should be interviewed. It is not necessary to interview every witness if the information is duplicative, unless you uncover conflicting accounts. The same approach should be taken in interviewing witnesses identified by the alleged wrongdoer.

When to interview the alleged wrongdoer
Generally, the witnesses identified by the complainant should be interviewed before the alleged wrongdoer. If, for some reason, it is impossible to interview the complainant's witnesses first, the investigator should be prepared to interview them without delay after interviewing the alleged wrongdoer.

Generally, the alleged wrongdoer should not be notified of the complaint before he or she is interviewed. However, if the allegations are against a senior executive, it may be necessary to notify the executive that a claim has been made against him or her and that an investigation will be conducted, but the executive should be told few details of the complaint at this point, and should be reminded of the company's policy against retaliation. The executive should also be directed not to discuss the allegation with the complainant or anyone else, and should be assured that the claim will be investigated promptly, professionally, and fairly. If a company elects to notify the alleged wrongdoer at the outset, it must be prepared to move forward with the investigation despite possible protest from the alleged wrongdoer, and must do so without interference from the alleged wrongdoer.

Regardless of when the alleged wrongdoer is interviewed, he or she should **not** be provided with a copy of the written complaint, if any, or specific details of the claim. Certainly, the investigator will need to provide the specific details of the allegations when interviewing the alleged wrongdoer, but that should be done during the course of the interview, not before.

Conducting the investigation

Third-party witnesses

Witnesses should be informed that a co-worker has brought a complaint and that the witness has been identified as someone who may have relevant information about the complaint. Explain that the information he or she provides will be kept confidential to the extent possible, and remind the employee of the company's policy against retaliation. At the outset, the investigator should obtain general information about the witness's relationship with the complainant and with the alleged wrongdoer, and general information about the witness's knowledge of the relationship between the complainant and the alleged wrongdoer. The investigator should also determine whether the complainant ever talked with the witness about the allegations in the complaint, and should inquire into the witness's knowledge of the specific allegations in detail.

Obviously the questions should be designed to obtain facts, but should also allow the investigator to evaluate the witness's credibility, which may involve asking questions for which the investigator already knows the answer. The investigator may also need to ask about specific details relating to the allegations in the claim, which standing alone may not be important or relevant, but may allow the investigator to corroborate other witnesses' statements. The witness should be asked to refrain from discussing the investigation with any other party.

Interview of the alleged wrongdoer

As with any alleged wrongdoer, but certainly with a senior executive, it is important to begin the interview in a non-confrontational manner. Begin the interview by explaining the investigation process and asking general questions about how the alleged wrongdoer knows the complainant and about the nature of their interactions before moving into more specific and sensitive areas. While it will be necessary to ask direct, difficult and, at times, confrontational, perhaps embarrassing questions, they need not, and should not be asked in an accusatory or offensive manner.

In general, the rules that apply to third-party witnesses apply to the alleged wrongdoer as well. However, unlike third-party witnesses, the alleged wrongdoer must be provided with the specific details of each and every allegation made against him or her so that he or she has the opportunity to refute or otherwise respond fully to each allegation. The investigator should go through each allegation individually and ask the alleged wrongdoer to respond. If he or she denies the allegation, ask if he or she engaged in any similar conduct with the complainant, and ask if the alleged wrongdoer knows of any reason why the complainant would have made the allegation if it were not true.

You should also obtain the names of potential witnesses who the alleged wrongdoer believes could support his or her version of the facts and/or provide other relevant information. If the alleged wrongdoer admits to the conduct, find out how the complainant reacted or responded at the time.

As with third-party witnesses, it is important to ask questions that will help evaluate the alleged wrongdoer's credibility on the subject and the investigator must not be swayed by his or her prior opinion of the alleged wrongdoer, but should make every effort to ensure that the information is being evaluated fairly.

Reaching a conclusion and completing the investigation

After completing the interviews, the investigator must consider the witness statements, evaluate the credibility of the witnesses, consider possible motivation to be dishonest or less than truthful, and must ultimately reach a conclusion as to what did or did not occur. Those conclusions and the bases for those conclusions must then be communicated to the appropriate decision-makers to determine what, if any, action is appropriate based upon the investigator's conclusions.

Whether those conclusions should be put into a written report will depend on the nature of the allegations, and the surrounding facts and circumstances, and should be discussed in advance with the company's general counsel and/or outside counsel. It is important to keep in mind, however, that any written investigation report will generally be discoverable, meaning it would need to be produced to the government agency or the plaintiff in the event that an external charge or lawsuit is filed. In most instances, the company will want to produce the report if a claim or lawsuit is filed to demonstrate that it took the complaint seriously, conducted a thorough, fair, and timely investigation, and took appropriate action based upon the results of the investigation.

In some instances involving senior executives, the company, upon advice of counsel, may decide to have counsel conduct the investigation in order for the investigation to be subject to the protection of the attorney-client privilege. Deciding whether to use the attorney-client privilege, and how to do so effectively, should be discussed in advance with the general counsel and/or outside counsel.

Once the investigation is complete, and the decision has been made as to what action, if any, is to be taken, the investigator should meet with the complainant to review the results of the investigation. The review should not go into great detail as to the investigator's specific findings, but rather provide an overall conclusion. If wrongdoing has been found, the complainant should be informed that appropriate action will be taken to correct the problem and ensure that it does not happen again (assuming, of course, that some action has been or will be taken). Again, the complainant should be reminded of the company's policy against retaliation and should be encouraged to report any future concerns.

A company that takes all claims of discrimination and harassment seriously, conducts a prompt, fair and thorough investigation whenever a complaint is received, and takes prompt remedial action when appropriate will help create a positive and productive work environment and will generally provide the company with an effective defense in any subsequent litigation. Conversely, a cursory or incomplete investigation will often form the basis for an employee's claim that the company knew or should have known of the unlawful conduct and that it failed to take appropriate action. Your company will be well served by following these general rules and taking the time to plan for any investigation.

Chapter 3

Managing Employee Leaves of Absence

Ann Robins, Axiom

The legal rights and obligations governing or affecting various types of employee absences from work (medical and otherwise) have fundamentally changed over the past several years into a tangled web of unrelated, overlapping, sometimes inconsistent legal requirements. This chapter emphasizes the need for employers to conduct a comprehensive review of company policies, handbook provisions, practices and procedures relating to leaves of absence to ensure that company policies and practices are updated as needed to comply with applicable laws. A checklist to facilitate the review is also included.

Overview

Until recently, employers were relatively free to establish and enforce their own terms and conditions governing absences from work, including whether and how much time off (if any) would be allowed per year for sick days, holidays, vacation, etc., and to what extent (if any) time off would be paid or unpaid. However, in today's increasingly regulated and complex workplace, consistent enforcement of many commonplace attendance policies often violates federal and state laws. Complicated and overlapping sets of rules require every absence—especially medical-related requests for time off—to be scrutinized under applicable "absence entitlement" or "absence accommodation" regimes. Given the recent statutory and regulatory changes, as well as guidance and interpretative materials issued by the EEOC, employers are well advised to conduct a comprehensive review of all policies, handbook provisions, practices, and procedures relating to managing employee absences.

Below is a checklist for facilitating such a review. Upon identifying the issues, employers should work with human resources and legal counsel to further assess and update absence management-related policies as appropriate.

1. **Identify/gather the various policies/employee handbook provisions relating to absences from work.**

Although practices vary, you may find rules and processes relating to employee absences dispersed among various policy contexts, including non-pension related employer provided benefits (e.g., time off for illness or childcare; bereavement leave; salary continuation or short-time disability/medical leaves; sabbatical, educational or other personal leaves of absence); employee rules of conduct (process for calling in if reporting late for, or too ill to work); disciplinary rules (consequences for unexcused absences); and time off to perform public services (military service, jury duty, time off for voting, etc.). *Consider consolidating all absence-related provisions into one well-organized and easy to use reference.*

2. **Formally withdraw or cancel (making a written record and following your internal procedures) any policies or handbook provisions that have been superseded in whole or part, no longer reflect current practices, or fail to meet current legal requirements.**

Have any categories lost relevance, become obsolete, or represent positions inconsistent with current values/leadership? Have technological changes affected the policy or process? Is the language still current and meaningful?

3. **Review your policy to ensure compliance with the "Injured Service Member Leave Act"[4] amendment to the Family and Medical Leave Act of 1993 (FMLA) and the reissued Final FMLA Regulations (which became effective January 2009).**

---

[4] Section 585(a) of the National Defense Authorization Act for Fiscal Year 2008 is also known as the "Injured Service Member Leave" amendment to the FMLA, which provides leave for qualifying exigencies for eligible family members of personnel on active duty and leave to care for ill or injured service members.

- The Injured Service Member Leave Act provides that eligible employees are entitled to:
  ◇ 12 workweeks of unpaid leave for any qualifying exigency arising out of the fact that the employee's spouse, son, daughter, or parent is on active duty or has been notified of an impending call or order to active duty in the U.S. National Guard or Reserves in support of a contingency operation; and
  ◇ 26 workweeks of leave during a single 12-month period to care for a covered service member with a serious injury or illness if the employee is the spouse, son, daughter, parent, or next of kin of the service member (Military Caregiver Leave)

4. **Review policy content for compliance with any applicable state or local legal requirements relating to employee time off/leaves of absence.**

Examples from the Washington, D.C., metropolitan region:

- *Maryland Flexible Leave Act:* Covers employers with 15 or more employees; employee has the right to use accrued sick or vacation leave for his/her own illness or to care for a child, spouse, and parent.
- *District of Columbia Family and Medical Leave Act:* If employee and employer are covered, employee has the right to up to 16 weeks of protected leave if illness qualifies as a "serious health condition."
- *District of Columbia Accrued Sick and Safe Leave Act:* Employees are entitled to accrue paid leave at the rate of 1 hour for a specified number of hours worked, not to exceed a total number of specified days allowed to be accrued per year. The accrual rates and annual maximums depend on the size of the employer (i.e., the number of employees). Employee cannot use accrued sick leave until employed for at least 90 days.

5. **Protected time off laws in the Washington, D.C., metropolitan area include the following (all of these laws are subject to additional terms and allow exception for undue hardship for the employer):**

- The District of Columbia requires time off for Emancipation Day (April 16) and "school activities."
- Maryland allows protected time off for crime victim proceedings.

- Virginia allows protected time off for crime victim proceedings, jury duty, and election officer duty.

6. **Work with legal counsel to draft a provision that clarifies that the employer intends to fully comply with all applicable laws and regulations and reserves the right to grant deviations to the policy under limited conditions as appropriate to ensure full legal compliance.**

The point here is to allow discretionary review under limited conditions in the event that a leave of absence might be viewed as a necessary reasonable accommodation under the ADA. Describe the process for seeking or granting deviations, and identify an executive position with authority to review and approve deviation requests.

Conclusion

Far from a comprehensive review of issues to be addressed in the course of updating or developing a plan for managing employee leaves of absence, this chapter identifies some of the more recent absence management issues that should be assessed, compared to, and considered together with an employer's existing absence management structure. The goal is to build a business—and employee-friendly program for managing absences, rooted in a legally compliant (and beyond) foundation with sufficient flexibility to allow for fair and effective administration with minimal uncertainty or pain.

Chapter 4

Six Essential Rules for Giving Feedback to Employees

By Ann Robins, Axiom

Persons holding managerial or supervisory positions are responsible for evaluating employee performance, usually through formal appraisals conducted annually or on another periodic review cycle, and through constructive feedback provided informally on a day-to-day basis. This chapter provides a brief summary of six essential rules for effectively communicating appraisal information and providing constructive feedback.

1. Be fair and respectful, prepared and professional.

You owe the employee the best guidance you can give. This means being prepared for the feedback session—don't wing it—and being ready to answer any questions and walk through any process to be implemented in connection with the performance review. Refresh your knowledge in advance of the meeting to ensure you have firm command of the key facts. Assume that everything the employee says to you is important information. Listen and take notes, especially noting ideas or suggestions raised by the employee.

2. Performance feedback should be fact-oriented and objective rather than subjective conclusions.

This requires preparation. For example, if the employee has had trouble learning new software, you should be prepared to discuss specific problems that you or others have encountered relating to the employee's software deficiency. Ask the employee for his ideas regarding what he needs for improvement and genuinely consider his ideas. However, it's also important for the manager to have at least two suggestions based on his/her experience and research.

Check facts and check them again if you need to, particularly if your discussion involves your reliance on a report prepared by someone else or perhaps an account of events described by another employee. Gut check your message in advance—is it the product of sound reasoning and supported by documented evidence? Always ask for the employee's input, side of the story, concerns, and questions.

3.   Be direct, concise, and accurate. (Say what you mean, and only what you mean.)

Don't sugarcoat (play down the importance of the constructive criticism) or embellish (exaggerate in the employee's favor). Short sentences are the most direct and effective. Adjectives are often unnecessary and prone to cause trouble down the road. After you've communicated your message, stop talking. Silence is acceptable. If your message is negative, do not throw in positive (likely insincere) filler to make things more comfortable. Embellishments have a long and often unproductive shelf life. Comfort is probably not a realistic goal in this situation, which is another good reason to keep it brief. If it helps, write down your feedback beforehand and, if necessary, read from your written notes.

4.   Take responsibility for the decision and the message. You own it—don't blame others.

As a manager, you speak for the company. If the company has made a decision on a matter that needs to be communicated to your direct reports, then you should be expected to carry out the communication without qualification—the same as if it were your decision. If you cannot do so, then discuss the issue with your chain of management so that they can make alternate arrangements for communicating to your direct reports.

5.   Never give corrective or negative feedback in public (no exceptions) or in the presence of other employees.

Criticizing your direct reports in the presence of other employees will sabotage the effectiveness and reduce the legitimacy of what you intended as an important, constructive message. Your employee will long remember the humiliation, anger or embarrassment he experienced and probably will not recall the constructive comments. Other employees or bystanders will, likewise, remember the vicarious experience of humiliation and/or sympathy for the employee rather than your insightful observations.

6. If you are angry or emotional, step away, take a walk, delay the discussion and let things cool off.

Similar to negative feedback in front of others, a show of unbridled anger will defeat your message and possibly seriously derail your career. The takeaway message or memory of an inappropriate display of emotions will trump the message or lesson. The point you are trying to make—which might be quite important given the emotions involved—will be forgotten. Additionally, words communicated in anger are rarely as articulate or meaningful as a conversation taking place under calmer circumstances. Finally, anger or emotional outbursts are simply inappropriate and unbecoming in a work setting.

Conclusion

Although the above list contains six essential rules for giving feedback, the list is by no means intended to be exhaustive. The important take-aways are to establish (even memorize) ground rules for your conversation; study the situation and review it again; assess the facts and information, and then assess your assessment; give the discussion more advance thought and planning than you think you can give it, and prepare more than you think you need to.

Notes

Chapter 5

Assessing Termination Risks— a Checklist for Employers

By Ann Robins, Axiom

The purpose of this chapter is to provide a list of factors to consider in developing a fair and legally compliant termination review process.

Overview

The most important issues to consider when evaluating the possible termination of an employee are the substantive, fact-based, performance-related reasons supporting possible discharge and triggering the pre-termination review. Of comparable importance, but sometimes overlooked by management, is conducting an assessment of certain risks associated with terminating an employee that may or may not be related to the more visible facts giving rise to the proposed termination.

This chapter outlines a process in the form of a list of questions seeking responsive information that is likely to be relevant to the termination review and risk assessment. The checklist will prove of little use without responsive information obtained from a good faith review of an employer's records. The employer will find that not all checklist questions are relevant to every termination review and that responsive information may not exist for every question.

Termination risks to be reviewed

Employers should conduct a thorough search of company records, including any complaint databases and employee hotline logs, to identify the following:

- Whether the subject employee has ever made or been the subject of allegations made by others with respect to any of the following: an internal or public/external complaint of any kind alleging harassment, discrimination, OSHA violations, wage and hour violations, fraud, violation of the company's code of ethics and business conduct or other policies, workers compensation, unemployment compensation, or any violation of federal, state, or local laws or regulations.
  ◇ If so, what was the nature of the complaint, investigation, and outcome? Was the employee apprised of the outcome?
  ◇ Do any complaints make allegations against or otherwise relate to the management team involved in the potential termination?
  ◇ Did the nature of any complaint allege inappropriate behavior in the workplace, unlawful environmental or safety violations, or possible illegal activity in the workplace?
- Has the employee ever claimed a disability? Ever inquired about reasonable accommodation? Any records of accommodation or attempted accommodation of a disability?
  ◇ If so, has the company either accommodated or attempted to accommodate the employee's disability? Is there a written record of these issues, including attempts by the company to accommodate?
- Has the employee been on military leave in the past 2 years? How long was the leave? How much time has elapsed since the employee's return? (Ascertain whether the employee is entitled to layoff protection under the Uniformed Services Employment and Reemployment Rights Act (USERRA) and if so, for how long.)
- Is the employee currently on a medical leave of absence (LOA)? What is the nature and duration of the medical LOA? Has the employee taken leave in the past 12 months to care for a family member with a medical condition? Does employee have rights under the Injured Service Member Leave Act by virtue of employee or a family member's service in the military? Has the employee taken a non-medical, non-Family Medical Leave Act (FMLA)-related LOA in the last 12 months? What is the nature and duration of that LOA? Has employee/employee's spouse had a baby, adopted a child, or become a foster parent in the past 12 months? Does the employee volunteer for national emergencies (such as hurricanes, earthquake relief, etc.)? Have any requests for LOA for any purpose been

denied in the past 4 years? Assess any state family medical leave act laws and any federal FMLA issues (including the recent amendments and changes to the regulations). Assess any potential rights or benefits under any company-sponsored short or long term disability insurance or benefit plans. Has the employee ever tried to exercise rights under such plans that have been denied in whole or part?

- Is the employee's employment subject to an employment contract? If so, review all relevant terms.

- Is the employee out on workers compensation leave? Has the employee ever been injured on the job? Has the employee ever been out on workers compensation in the past 4 years? Has the employer ever denied workers compensation benefits, or have such benefits ever been the subject of dispute by the employee? Has the employee ever filed an appeal or sought review of a workers compensation claim? What is the status of any pending workers compensation claims?

- Has the employee ever participated in any legal proceedings (including arbitrations and mediation sessions) involving the company? If so, what was the nature of such proceedings, and what role did the employee play in the proceeding? Has the employee's deposition ever been taken in the case?

- Does the employee have any rights to full or partial payment under any employment or retention agreements in connection with work performed to date? Are there any other contracts that might trigger an obligation of the company to provide severance payments or other post-termination benefits to the employee?

- Has the employee signed any non-compete agreements, proprietary information or nondisclosure agreements, assignments of patents or other intellectual property, or any other agreement relating to trade secrets, confidential information, or intellectual property? Review these agreements for obligations or other terms and conditions that might be affected by employment termination.

- Is the employee about to reach a major benefit or compensation related milestone? Consider whether options (such as extending the employee's termination date by a very short period of time) might alleviate unintended harsh consequences and avoid unnecessary claims in litigation.

- Consider the pros and cons of negotiating an exit package, severance, or other termination agreement involving the payment of a lump sum (in an amount greater than the employee would otherwise be entitled to) in exchange for a valid waiver/release of claims. Even if the employee is under 40 years of age, employers should follow the requirements set forth in the Older Worker Benefit Protection Act (OWBPA) applicable to individual terminations. The EEOC has taken the position that a valid release of any discrimination-related claims must meet the fairly strict criteria set forth in the OWBPA.

- Follow all applicable state and local legal requirements relating to the payment amount (no improper deductions) and the timing and method of delivery of the employee's final paycheck, sometimes called "termination pay." Many state laws require employers to abide by special rules only applicable to termination pay. For example, some states require that paychecks be hand delivered on the final day of work, even if the employer had been paying by direct deposit. Check with legal counsel before deducting sums from the final paycheck as an offset for uniforms, computers, or other equipment that may have been lost (or even stolen) by the employee.

- Is the employer aware of any drug or alcohol problems involving the employee? Or any anger management issues? Domestic violence allegations or incidents? Any incidents relating to the use, possession, or purchase of guns or other weapons? Seek assistance from appropriate medical, law enforcement, security, or other professionals if issues are discovered that fall within these categories. The issues identified in this item must be reviewed in light of applicable laws governing certain types of protected information. Such protected information may include, for example, criminal records (arrest, conviction, expungement, minor status) and protected personal data or private information (expectation of privacy issues, information obtained via surveillance, protected medical-related information, and the like). Employers should comply with any legal prohibitions relating to accessing or considering certain types of protected information.

Conclusion

Employment relationships are terminated for various reasons, ranging from involuntary layoffs due to lack of work and no fault of the employee to "for cause" terminations involving theft or workplace violence. The most important factor in any decision to terminate employment is the legitimacy of the reason for termination. The facts must lead one to this reason for termination without embellishment or manipulation of facts or gaps in them. The information gathered pursuant to this checklist should not be used for or related to justifying a termination. Rather, the information gathered and considered pursuant to the suggestions in this chapter should be used to assess risks associated with any termination in order to help avoid costly and unpleasant consequences.

Notes

Chapter 6

Potentially Costly Wage and Hour Mistakes Employers Make During Tough Economic Times

By Ann Robins, Axiom

This chapter addresses certain potentially costly wage and hour mistakes commonly made by employers. These mistakes are somewhat more likely to occur when competing in a tough competitive market or confronting periods of economic downturn, and include making improper deductions from the salaries of exempt employees during furlough periods and other management actions to cut costs such as banning overtime, or asking employees to work off the clock, among others.

Background

In spite of being among the oldest employment-related laws (enacted in 1938), the Fair Labor Standards Act (FLSA) collective (class) actions represent the largest and fastest growing area of employment litigation, growing 44 percent from 2008 to 2009.

All employees fall into one of two categories under the FLSA:

1) *exempt*: those who fall within one of the statutory exemptions, and therefore, are not covered by the FLSA's minimum wage and overtime requirements; and
2) *non-exempt employees:* those who do not fall within the categories covered by the FLSA exemptions.

The FLSA establishes minimum wage, overtime pay, record keeping, and child labor requirements. Subject to certain exemptions, such as the so-called "white collar" exemption discussed below, the FLSA and associated Department of Labor (DOL) regulations require employers to pay all non-exempt employees at least the federal minimum wage (currently, $7.25 per hour) plus overtime pay (an hourly rate of at least 1.5 times the regular rate) for hours worked in excess of 40 hours in a workweek.

Notably, the FLSA does not require employers to provide breaks for meal or rest periods, time off for sick leave, or vacation days or premium pay for holidays or special shifts; however, many states and local authorities impose their own wage and hour laws addressing such obligations. So long as state and local governments' laws exceed federal requirements, the FLSA allows those jurisdictions to impose additional, even conflicting wage and hour obligations, such as mandating periodic break periods for rest or meals, applying different rules for calculating overtime pay, or establishing higher minimum wage rates. For example, the minimum wage in the District of Columbia is $8.25 per hour, a dollar more than the federal minimum hourly rate.

Damages/penalties for FLSA violations

If a plaintiff (including the DOL) prevails on an FLSA claim for failure to pay minimum wage, for example, or for overtime hours worked but not paid, the plaintiff is awarded, and the employer must pay, damages equal to the unpaid wages or overtime.

Under these circumstances, the court ordinarily assesses liquidated damages (2 × actual damages) against the employer as well. Note that individual supervisors can be held personally liable for FLSA violations. Liquidated damages (double damages) are not considered punitive under the FLSA, but rather as part of compensatory damages to make the employee whole for the delay in payment of wages owed under the law. Therefore, generally, an award of liquidated damages under the FLSA is *mandatory* unless the employer can show good faith and reasonable grounds for believing that it was not in violation of the FLSA.

Common mistakes

Mistake #1: Failure to adhere to the "salary basis" rules by making improper deductions from the pay of salaried exempt employees.
Potential consequence: Can jeopardize the employee's exempt status and expose the employer to liability for overtime wages.

The categories of potentially exempt positions described in the FLSA—bona fide executive, professional, administrative, outside sales, and certain computer services—are often casually referenced as the "white collar" exemptions, an unfortunate and misleading label. Although some individuals who happen to work in an office or white-collar work environment may qualify as "exempt" employees due to the specific nature of their job duties, it is equally as likely that a substantial number of office employees in any given workplace are accurately classified as non-exempt under the FLSA based on their respective job duties.

This chapter does not attempt to cover the complex analyses required to properly classify employees as exempt or nonexempt under the FLSA (and comparable state laws), but it should be noted that "white collar" (related to work in an office setting) is not particularly useful information when determining which employees in a firm with 100 office workers are exempt and which are not. Employers should work with their legal counsel and human resources professionals to periodically review FLSA compliance by conducting the necessary duty-based job analyses, and taking steps as appropriate (adjusting duties or reclassifying, for example) to ensure that employees are properly classified for minimum wage and overtime purposes.

In addition to satisfying the job duty requirements, "exempt" employees must meet the "salary basis test" to qualify as exempt. To be exempt, the employee must: 1) earn a salary level of at least $455 per week; 2) be paid on a "salary basis," which means the employee must receive a set amount of compensation each pay period which is not subject to reduction regardless of the quality or quantity of the work performed; and 3) be paid a full salary for any week in which the employee performs any work (but the employee need not be paid for any workweek when no work is performed).

Failure to adhere to the "salary basis" rules by making improper deductions from pay can jeopardize the employee's exempt status and expose the employer to liability for overtime wages. Depending on the facts associated with the employer's improper claim of exempt status, liability for unpaid overtime can include overtime hours worked by the employee during a look-back period of up to 2 or, in some cases, 3 years.

Furloughs—an example of improper deductions from pay of exempt employees: A furlough is a short-term cost cutting strategy used by employers usually involving an involuntary, temporary, unpaid reduction in employee work hours. In tough economic times, employers may see furloughs as an option to cut costs without terminating employees, but must exercise caution when furloughs involve exempt employees.

- Unpaid furloughs of exempt employees must be in full week increments. (Avoid deductions for partial day or partial week absences.)
- Advise exempt employees that absolutely no work can be performed during furloughed time off. Working during furloughs could jeopardize exempt status. Take away BlackBerries and laptops to avoid temptations. Assure exempt employees that any pending assignments or deadlines are on hold until the furlough is over. Confirm this with all managers. Furloughed exempt employees facing upcoming post-furlough deadlines may feel compelled to secretly work at home during furlough.
- Another option: Employers can send exempt employees home without pay in any increments and require them to use available paid leave to make up the lost salary as long as they receive a full paycheck for the pay period. What about vacation leave? It's permissible under FLSA to require employees to use vacation leave during furloughs, but the practice may not be legal under some state laws.
- Perhaps unpopular, but another legal option is for the employer to permanently reduce the employee's salary, provided (a) the salary is not reduced below the threshold "salary basis" amount of $455 per week, (b) the number of hours to be worked is not dictated by the employer, and (c) other "salary basis" rules are followed, as set forth in previous section. Do not use this option as an attempt to pay exempt employees like hourly employees. Finally, FLSA regulations require strict scrutiny of the frequency of salary and schedule changes for exempt employees. Frequent salary changes that suggest an employer is attempting to treat the salary as the functional equivalent of an hourly wage can invalidate the exemption and lead to back pay liability for unpaid overtime worked by employees previously considered exempt.
- Agreements signed by employees authorizing improper deductions are prohibited by FLSA, unenforceable, and will not preserve the exemption. Don't try it.

Employers can limit their liability by incorporating a "safe harbor" prohibiting improper claims of exemptions from FLSA.

If an employer violates the "salary basis" and improperly claims an exemption for payments to which an employee is entitled, the DOL regulations set forth a "safe harbor" provision that, if properly implemented, still may limit an employer's exposure to liability. To qualify under the safe harbor, an employer must meet all of the following requirements:

1) Have a "clearly communicated" policy prohibiting improper exemptions and setting forth a specific complaint mechanism for employees to follow to challenge exemption status or improper deductions. The policy should be in writing with notice and access to employees. Be sure the policy articulates the prohibited deductions so that employees have adequate notice of why, how, and when to follow the complaint process.

2) Upon learning of improper deductions, reimburse employees in a timely manner; and

3) Make a good faith commitment to comply in the future (and make sure improper deductions cease after receipt of employee complaints). Educate management, including Human Resources. Keep up to date with the law, and modify policies and practices to ensure ongoing compliance.

Mistake #2: Adopting a ban on all overtime. Refusing to pay overtime unless requested by management and approved in advance.

Potential consequence: Intimidated and worried about keeping their jobs, nonexempt employees may decide not to report extra hours worked. As a result, the employer violates FLSA's recordkeeping and overtime pay requirements

Scenario: The manager is focused on the budget, which is tight and getting tighter. Reviewing a spreadsheet of costs, it's clear that overtime costs add up—_even if it's only a handful of employees staying an extra 15 or 20 minutes a day to wrap things up._ The manager decides to ban all overtime unless requested and approved in advance. An overtime ban, in and of itself, does not violate wage and hour laws. It depends on the facts.

- It's acceptable to limit overtime and instruct managers not to ask or allow employees to work overtime.
- However, any overtime hours worked by non-exempt employees— including any time worked that was neither requested nor approved by the supervisor—must be paid in full. If the time is worked, the employer is obligated to pay—no matter what. This should be communicated to the employees. For example, "We are asking that you not work overtime hours unless requested to do so and approved in advance; if you need to work additional hours to meet your deadlines, advise us so that we can

adjust your workload. Notwithstanding the overtime cutback, if you work any hours beyond 40 in a workweek, you must record the time and you will be paid at your overtime rate;" etc.

- Be cautious when providing nonexempt employees with BlackBerries, laptops, and other remote access technology. These devices make working from home (even for 15-30 minutes) far more likely. When issuing remote access technology to non-exempt employees, employers should require employees to acknowledge in writing their obligation to record all working time, regardless of work location.
- Written policy should include a requirement that employees report all working time with no exceptions.

Mistake #3: Asking non-exempt (overtime eligible) employees to work "off the clock."

Potential consequence: Willful violation of FLSA's overtime requirements; also recordkeeping violations.

This is **never** acceptable.

Managers are responsible for making sure that all time worked by employees is properly recorded.

What if the employer offers to "make it up" to the worker or offers "comp time" in lieu of overtime pay? *Again, this is **never** acceptable.* The FLSA does not allow employees to waive their rights to receive minimum wage and applicable overtime pay for all hours worked. Any such agreement is void and unenforceable.

Non-exempt workers can only be provided with compensatory time in lieu of overtime if: 1) comp time is taken during the same pay period in which it is accrued and 2) the employee receives one-and-one-half hours of comp time for each hour of overtime. Providing nonexempt employees with tools such as email, text messaging, BlackBerries, and smart phones increases the risks for off-the-clock work by making it easy to stay connected after work hours and on weekends.

Mistake #4: Incorrect treatment of breaks and meal periods.

Potential consequence: FLSA violation for failure to properly pay for all compensable time; possible recordkeeping violations.

Although the FLSA does not require rest or meal periods, it does require that any employer-provided rest or meal periods from 5 to 20 minutes in duration must be counted as compensable working time. (Recall that state laws often require rest or meal periods; the FLSA "compensable time" rule for breaks up to 20 minutes applies regardless of whether a break period is mandated by state law or voluntarily provided by the employer.)

- Under the FLSA, meal periods are non-working (non-compensable) time if they last 30 minutes or more *and* if the employee is completely relieved of duties. However, if the employer voluntarily provides meal or rest break periods in an employee handbook, written policy, employee agreement, or employee contract, and if the employer fails to provide the prescribed break or meal periods, employees can pursue FLSA and other types of claims seeking payment for breaks that were promised, but not provided or properly compensated.

- Check your employee handbooks/company policies/employee contracts for outdated provisions, paying special attention to any provisions referencing break/meal periods.
  - ◇ In two separate class action cases against Wal-Mart (one in Texas, another in New Jersey), classes of employees brought suit for breach of contract and wage and hour violations because employees had been given outdated versions of employee handbooks which contained provisions for rest and meal periods that Wal-Mart claimed were no longer valid. Although the meal and rest periods described in the handbook had never been provided to, used by, or requested by these employees, Wal-Mart was bound by the terms of the employee handbook that provided for meal and rest periods.

Mistake #5: Improper record keeping.

Potential consequence: Assume an employee files a complaint with the DOL or pursues litigation seeking payment for overtime worked, but not paid. If the employer denies that an employee worked hours for which she was not paid, the employer has the burden to produce records that prove the hours worked. If records do not exist to support the employer's claim, the employee's claim of hours worked will be presumed to be true by a court.

Employers must maintain the following detailed information for all non-exempt employees:

- regular hourly rate;
- total hours worked per day;
- total hours worked per week;
- straight time earnings for the first 40 hours per week;
- payments excluded from the regular rate of pay;
- weekly overtime payments.

Note that some states have differing and additional recordkeeping requirements.

Conclusion

Special wage and hour compliance challenges await employers trying to survive or remain competitive, especially during periods of economic recession or hardship. The issues addressed in this chapter represent a sample of the many potentially costly wage and hour mistakes commonly made by employers in bad times, or even good.

SECTION VIII
ACCOUNTING AND TAX TIPS

CONTENTS

Chapter 1

Overview of Technology Tax Incentives

Joyce M. Robinson, Argy, Wiltse & Robinson, P.C.[5]

By offering a wide range of services including consulting and engineering services, IT support, software programming, and hardware construction, technology companies often run the gamut from incurring huge losses to earning colossal profits.

In order to balance out some of the expenses and encourage technology companies to produce income and jobs in their jurisdictions, many different taxing authorities offer incentives to technology firms. This chapter briefly outlines some of the available tax incentives in the Northern Virginia area.

1. Federal tax incentives

Research and development (R&D) credit
The R&D credit is targeted to urge businesses to increase spending on research and development activities

Two methods available for calculation: regular credit, and alternative simplified credit.

- The regular credit is generally 20 percent of the increase in R&D spending over a base period amount. The base period amount looks at a ratio of qualified research expenses (QRE) to gross receipts over the 1984 to 1988 period. If the company had no QRE during that period, then a fixed percentage is assigned.

---

[5]   Lance Louderback and Stuart Fox of Argy, Wiltse & Robinson, P.C., also contributed to this chapter.

- The alternative simplified credit equals 14 percent of the excess of current year QREs over 50 percent of the taxpayer's average QREs for the prior 3 years. Companies that do not qualify for the regular credit often qualify for alternative simplified credit.

The credit offsets taxes owed or paid. If the company does not have a tax liability then the R&D credit may be carried forward for up to 20 years.

Expensing of internally developed software costs and research and development expenses.

The taxpayer may elect to expense or capitalize and amortize internally developed software costs and research and development expenses. Once the election is made, the taxpayer may not change its method unless a Form 3115 is completed to change methods.

2. Virginia tax incentives

Technology zones

Qualified technology companies that operate in technology zones may receive various incentives.

Technology zone incentives may include waiving of local permit and user fees, local tax exemptions, and special zoning treatment.

Virginia has 24 technology zones established in the state, including Arlington and Falls Church in the Northern Virginia region. Go to *yesvirginia.org* to find out if you are located within a technology zone.

Fairfax County Business Professional Occupational License (BPOL) exemptions

Qualified technology companies may be allowed certain exclusions from the BPOL gross receipts tax.

Technology companies focusing on software development may receive exclusions related to software sales, leases, or licensing.

Companies selling computer hardware or software to the government may be allowed to exclude costs sold under contract.

Sales and use tax exemptions for IT consulting to government entities

A wide range of companies are eligible for the exemptions, including manufacturers, distributors, software developers, purchasers, semiconductors, and many others.

3. District of Columbia tax incentives

High technology development zones

The New E-conomy Transformation Act of 2000 has defined certain areas of the District of Columbia as High Technology Development Zones. Go to *dcbiz.dc.gov* to find the zone locations.

Qualified high technology corporations (QHTCs) located within the zones are not required to pay any franchise tax for 5 years starting with the date that the QHTC commences business in the zone.

The franchise tax rate for qualified high tech corporations located outside of the zones is 6 percent.

Wages of up to $5,000 per employee hired may be reimbursed. Relocation expenses of $5,000 may be reimbursed for employees relocated to the District ($7,500 if the employee relocates his or her personal residence into the District).

Personal property tax exemptions

A 10-year exemption applies to qualified personal property purchased by a QHTC after December 31, 2000.

Sales and use tax exemptions

Sales to a QHTC of computer software or hardware and certain other technology equipment may be exempt from District sales tax.

QHTC's are exempt from sales and use tax on intangible property or service sales within the District. This exemption does not apply to telecommunication service providers.

Capital gains tax exemptions

Capital gains related to the sale or transfer of stock ownership and other assets of QHTC's held more than 5 years are not taxable.

4. Maryland tax incentives

Research and development tax credit
The basic R&D tax credit is 3 percent of eligible R&D expenses that do not exceed the company's average R&D expenses over a 4-year period.

A growth R&D tax credit is 10 percent of eligible R&D expenses that exceed the company's 4-year average of eligible R&D expenses.

This chapter summarizes many ways a technology company is able to save taxes. Even a start-up company can reduce costs by taking advantage of the tax incentives offered by the various jurisdictions. The tax incentives offered impact all taxes, including income, sales and use and personal property taxes.

The information contained within this article is current as of May 5, 2010. Please contact a licensed tax professional to verify there have been no tax law changes since the publishing of this article.

IRS Circular 230 disclosure: Please be advised that the tax advice contained herein (including any attachments) is not intended or written by the practitioner to be used and cannot be used by the taxpayer for the purpose of avoiding any U.S. tax-related penalties that may be imposed on the taxpayer.

Chapter 2

Top Things To Know About Business Systems

Paul M. Bailey, Argy, Wiltse & Robinson, P.C.

Contracting with the federal government requires business systems and methods of accounting to comply with government procurement rules, regulations and public law. The type of contract, value, and method of procurement all influence the specific requirements. Generally, government agencies follow the requirements established by the Department of Defense (DoD) and described in the DoD FAR Supplement. This chapter provides an overview of the business system requirements.

1. What business systems are required by the FAR?

Accounting system
- General standards require the contractor to have the necessary accounting and operational controls, or the ability to obtain them.
- The contracting officer determines system adequacy and suitability for use in administering the proposed contract type based on information obtained in part from the government auditor.
- A cost reimbursement contract may be used only when the accounting system is adequate for determining costs applicable to the contract.
- Fixed-price contracts may necessitate an accounting system to segregate the cost of changed work until an equitable adjustment is agreed.
- Standard Form 1408 lists accounting system expectations for cost-based contracts.

Earned value management system (FAR Subpart 34.2)
- Required for major acquisitions for development.

- Requires contractors to submit EVMS monthly reports for applicable contracts. An integrated baseline review verifies technical content and realism of related budgets, resources, and schedules.

Purchasing system (FAR Subpart 44.3)
- When a contract exceeds the simplified acquisition threshold, government consent to subcontract may be required based on the subcontract type (FP, CP, T&M), value, agency, source of supply, and services performed.
- Purchasing systems that are approved limit the instances where government consent is required.
- A contractor purchasing system review (CPSR) is generally performed when sales based on negotiated procurements to the government/prime are expected to exceed $25 million in the next 12 months.
- The objective of the CPSR is to evaluate the efficiency and effectiveness of spending government monies and complying with government policy when subcontracting.

Estimating systems (FAR Subpart 15.407-5)
- An acceptable system benefits both the government and contractor by increasing the accuracy and reliability of proposals.
- Approved systems may expedite proposal negotiation and lead to a competitive advantage.

Property management system (FAR Part 45)
- Systems designed to protect the government's interest in property and/or materials.

2. What business systems are required by the DoD FAR Supplement?

Accounting system
- Necessary for the following contract administration:
  ◇ Cost reimbursement, cost-based incentive, time-and-material, or labor hour contract
  ◇ Fixed price contract with progress payments based on cost incurred or percentage/stage of completion
  ◇ Construction contract that includes FAR clause 52.232-27, Prompt Payment for Construction Contracts.

Earned value management system (EVMS)
- Cost or incentive contracts and subcontracts valued at $20 million or more must comply with the guidelines of American National Standards Institute (ANSI)/Electronics Industry Alliance (EIA) Standard 748.
- Cost or incentive contracts and subcontracts valued at $50 million or more must have an EVMS that has been determined to be in compliance with ANSI/EIA-748
- EVMS adequacy is determined by the 32 criteria described in ANSI/EIA-748.

Purchasing system
- DFARS establishes additional considerations for system adequacy.

Estimating system
- Large businesses are subject to disclosure, maintenance, and review requirements if they received DoD prime contracts or subcontracts in the preceding fiscal year for which cost or pricing data were required:
  ◇ Totaling $50 million or more; or
  ◇ Totaling $10 million predominately government and the CO and ACO believe significant estimating problems exist.

Material management and accounting system (MMAS)
- Required of large, for profit businesses with $40 million government contract or subcontract sales in the preceding year where cost of pricing data was required.
- The contractor is subject to disclosure, maintenance, and system review for:
  ◇ Reasonableness of forecast material requirements,
  ◇ Charging of material costs to a contract based on valid time-phased requirements, and
  ◇ Maintaining consistent, equitable, and unbiased logic for costing of material transactions.

Property management system
- Prescribes policy and procedure for acquisition, use and rental, and disposal of government property.
- Permits physical comingling of inventories charged to contracts when MMAS requirements are met.

DoD proposed rule (Case 2009-D038)

Failure to maintain any element of the proposed six DoD systems leading to a deficiency will result in withholding of payments to the contractor. Penalties are cumulative by system.

Chapter 3

Top Things To Know About Pricing Government Awards

Sajeev Malaveetil, Argy, Wiltse & Robinson, P.C.

It is the federal government's pricing policy to obtain products and services from responsible sources at prices that are determined to be fair and reasonable. How a contracting officer goes about determining fair and reasonableness of a particular priced action will depend on a number of factors. This chapter summarizes how government contracts are priced and how a contractor's pricing is evaluated.

1. What impacts my pricing of a contract?

How a contract action is priced will depend heavily upon the nature of the goods or services being procured, the procurement method used, and the type of procurement issued.

Sealed bid awards

Goods and services purchased under a sealed-bid award typically have the least onerous pricing requirements. This is primarily a result of the nature of market competition. With adequate price competition, a contracting officer can reach a conclusion regarding fair and reasonable pricing without obtaining cost or pricing data.

- Sealed bid procurements tend to be used when the government requirements are well defined, and the product or service being procured is commonly available.
- Sealed bid procurements are often used for pricing the acquisition of commercial items.

- Price is typically the primary element of source selection in sealed bid awards.

Negotiated awards

In contrast to sealed bid awards, negotiated awards typically involve pricing that includes an analysis of price and/or cost. This is because negotiated awards may involve less competition.

- Negotiated procurements tend to be used when the government requirements are less defined and/or when the government is seeking the manufacturing of an item or research and developmental services.
- Price is typically one of several evaluation factors for source selection in negotiated procurements.

2. What type of data must I submit?

The amount of data that is required to be submitted with a price proposal will vary depending upon the same factors that influence how an action is priced (nature of product, procurement method used, and type of procurement issued).

Regardless, it is the government's pricing policy that a contracting officer, in determining whether prices are fair and reasonable, must not obtain more information than is necessary from the contractor.

Contracts requiring submission of cost or pricing data

"Cost or pricing data" is a unique term that refers to a specific classification of data that is submitted for certain negotiated contracts. Typically, cost or pricing data are required to be submitted for negotiated contracts that are above a specified dollar threshold (currently $650,000) and do not meet a set of exception criteria.

- The cost or pricing data, which are required to be accurate, complete, and current at the date of agreement on the contract/action price, serve as the basis upon which the government contracting officer makes a determination as to whether prices are fair and reasonable.
- When submitting cost or pricing data, a contractor must also submit a certification of current cost or pricing data, certifying that to the best of its knowledge and belief, the cost or pricing data were accurate, complete, and current as of the date of the agreed upon price.

- A false certification can result in future downward price adjustments and potentially other adverse consequences to the contractor.

Contracts not requiring submission of cost or pricing data

Cost or pricing data are not required to be submitted when any of several exceptions are met. These include acquisitions at or below the simplified acquisition threshold, instances where pricing is based on adequate price competition, instances where pricing is based on law or regulation, or when a commercial product or service is being acquired.

However, the government may require "information other than cost or pricing data" to support a determination of price reasonableness or cost realism. Any such data do not require certification.

3. What kind of price or cost analysis will be performed?

When cost or pricing data are required, the government will perform a cost analysis to evaluate the reasonableness of individual cost elements (labor, other direct costs, overhead, etc.) of a proposal, as well as a price analysis to ensure that the overall price offered is fair and reasonable.

When cost or pricing data are not required, the government will perform a price analysis to ensure that the overall price offered is fair and reasonable.

Price analysis

A price analysis may include one or more of the following techniques: a comparison of proposed prices to the solicitation requirements; a comparison of proposed prices to prior prices paid; an analysis of unit pricing; a comparison with published market prices; a comparison of proposed prices with independent government cost estimates; and a comparison of proposed prices to prices identified through market research.

Cost analysis

A cost analysis can include one or more of the following techniques: a verification of cost or pricing data and evaluation of cost elements; an evaluation of the effect of the offeror's current practices on future costs; a comparison of costs proposed by the offeror for individual cost elements with additional information; verification of compliance with the Cost Principles and Cost Accounting Standards; an evaluation of the adequacy of the data used to prepare the proposal; and an analysis of the results of any make-or-buy reviews by the contractor.

Profit analysis

Finally, the government will perform an analysis of profit using a structured approach that takes into consideration items such as performance risk, contract type risk, the extent to which facilities capital is employed, and cost efficiency.

Chapter 4

Top Things To Know About Accounting for Changes

Paul M. Bailey, Argy, Wiltse & Robinson, P.C.

1. How do I account for contract changes?

Changes within the general scope of the contract

- The contracting officer may make changes within the general scope of the contract that increase or decrease the cost or the time required to perform work. These include additions, deletions, and substitutions of work under the contract. Examples of changes that occur include drawings, designs, or specifications, method of shipment or packing, place of delivery, time of performance, schedule acceleration, and the amount of government-furnished property.

- The contractor is not required to incur costs for changes beyond the funded value of the contract.

- The contractor must assert its right to an adjustment of the contract within 30 days from the date of receipt of a written order. Failure to agree upon an adjustment is subject to the Disputes Clause of the contract.

Change order accounting

- When the change is estimated to exceed $100,000, the contracting officer may require the contractor to maintain separate accounts for the cost of both the changed and unchanged work.

- The value of the equitable adjustment for the changed work is based on the difference between the cost of performing the contract before and after the change.

- The price adjustment includes direct cost of added and deleted work not performed, indirect cost attributed to the modification, and profit/fee affected by the modification.

Administration
- The format of the request for equitable adjustment should be prepared in accordance with requirements at FAR Table 15-2.
- DoD requires certification for requests exceeding the simplified acquisition threshold.

2. What other types of changes impact contract value?

Other contract value changes may occur as a result of a change in cost accounting practices.

- A change in accounting practice may result from a change in measurement of cost, assignment to the accounting period, or allocation method.
- For contracts subject to the Cost Accounting Standards (CAS), verify which, if any, of the standards are applicable to the changed practice—"modified" (401, 402, 405, and 406) or "full coverage" (all standards).
- The change in contract value is measured against backlog from what was priced to that which would have been priced under the new method.
- Changes are aggregated by contract type (FP, T&M, CP, non-CAS) and evaluated for increases/decreases before netting.
- Post-award audits where cost or pricing data are required: Contract values may be adjusted for "defective" cost or pricing data, where it is shown that the cost or pricing data was not current, accurate, and complete at the time of certification (TINA—Truth in Negotiations Act).

Chapter 5

Top Things To Know About Revenue Recognition

Charlie Bonuccelli, Argy, Wiltse & Robinson, P.C.

Revenue is recognized based on the type of contract a contractor receives. The following is a summary of the top issues facing federal government contractors and does not represent a complete list of every issue that could arise.

1. When do I recognize revenue?

- Recognizing revenue on cost type contracts
  - ◇ Revenue is recognized under cost type contracts as cost is incurred (FASB Accounting Standards Codification 912-605-25-1). Differences resulting from adjustments or "true-up" to indirect rates (actual versus settled) are recognized in the year settled.
  - ◇ FASB Accounting Standards Codification 912-605-25-1 and 9 states that fixed fees may be proportionately recognized as it becomes billable, unless such fees are not proportionate to the work performed.
- Other contract types generally recognize revenue based upon a percentage of completion method. Codification effective July 1, 2009, while generally following AICPA Statement of Position (SOP)81-1 and AICPA Accounting Research Bulletin (ARB)45, supersedes them for revenue recognition on construction-type and production-type contracts. Codification 605-35-25 provides the criteria for measuring revenue. A percentage of completion method is based upon the cost incurred plus the estimated cost to completion (Consolidation 605-35-25-32). The main issues involving revenue recognition are:

◇ Combining or segmenting contracts for revenue reporting purposes is covered by Consolidation 605-35-8 through 14 that provide the criteria that need to be met. Where multiple contracts are so closely related that it is in essence one contract or for one customer, revenue recognition may be combined. A contract or group of contracts may be segmented where the profit levels, business unit performing the work, and project management vary within the project to develop revenue recognition that more closely reflects actual performance.

◇ Recognizing revenues on claims and change orders:
1) For approved change orders, the contract revenue and costs shall be adjusted (Codification 605-35-25-27).
2) For unpriced change orders not in dispute, the contractor may recognize revenue when there is customer acknowledgement of the change and reasonable basis for the value of the change order. All other unapproved change orders are to be evaluated as claims (Codification 605-35-25-28).
3) A claim may be recognized only when it is probable that the claim will result in additional revenue and there is a reliable estimate. These two conclusions are satisfied by meeting the following criteria found in Codification 605-35-25-31:
   a. There is a legal basis for the claim from the contract or from an independent legal opinion.
   b. Additional costs are due to unforeseen conditions and not due to poor contractor performance
   c. The additional cost can be identified or reasonably determined in view of the additional work to be performed.
   d. The evidence supporting the claim is objective and verifiable and not based on mere opinion or unsupported representations.

◇ Provisions for contract losses:
1) Consolidation 605-35-25-45 states that losses under contracts are to be recognized under GAAP as soon as they become evident.

2) Under the percentage of completion method of revenue recognition using an estimate to complete, the G&A is to be expensed as incurred (Consolidation 605-35-25-37).

2.   What balance sheet items should be considered?

Due to the complexities in the revenue recognition process for government contracts, a number of accounts may be created based on ARB 45 as described in the AICPA's Audit and Accounting Guide for federal government contractors (A&A Guide). Such guidance is not superseded by the FASB Accounting Standards Codification. The primary balance sheet accounts that contractors may deal with are:

- Costs in excess of billing and estimated earnings. This account captures the difference in the actual costs that were not yet billed because provisional indirect cost rates are too low.
- Billings in excess of cost and estimated earnings. Billings on cost type contracts for costs that are greater than actual cost incurred.
- Unbilled accounts receivable. This account captures the amounts recognized for revenue recognition purposes that have yet to be billed to the federal government.
- Advanced payments on contracts (deferred revenue). This account captures the amounts billed to the contract or advanced under FAR Part 32 in excess of revenues actually earned. Such amounts are repayable to the federal government until such time as revenues are earned or conditions are met that remove the repayment obligation.
- Provisions for contract losses. This account captures the accrued losses on contracts. The losses are amortized over the period of performance for the contract. This account is normally calculated annually based on the contract profit and loss analysis for the year-end revenue recognition

Notes

Chapter 6

Top Things To Know About Record Retention and Access to Records

Michael LaCorte, Argy, Wiltse & Robinson, P.C.

Federal government contractors are required to retain records for specified periods of time in order to meet the records review requirements of the government. This chapter provides an overview of record retention and access to records requirements for government contractors.

1. What records am I required to keep?

FAR Subpart 4.7—Contractor Records Retention, governs contractor records retention requirements for contractors with contracts containing either clause 52.214-26, Audit and Records—Sealed Bidding, or clause 52.215-2, Audit and Records—Negotiation. Records include books, documents, accounting procedures and practices, and other data, regardless of type and regardless of whether such items are in written form, in the form of computer data, or in any other form.

Contractors are generally required to keep such records for a period of three years after final contract payment, unless a longer retention period is contractually stipulated, the contractor does not meet the original due date for submission of final indirect cost rate proposals, or the specific class of record is statutorily subject to a different retention period.

Certain records may be statutorily subject to different retention requirements. Records retention requirements for the following classes of records are different than the 3 years prescribed in FAR Subpart 4.703(a)(1).

Financial and cost accounting records—FAR Part 4, Subpart 4.705-1

- Accounts receivable invoices, adjustments to the accounts, invoice registers, carrier freight bills, shipping orders, and other documents which detail materials or services billed on the related invoices are to be maintained for a period of 4 years.
- Material, work order, or service order files, consisting of purchase requisitions or purchase orders for materials or services, or orders for transfer of material or supplies, are to be maintained for a period of 4 years.
- Cash advance recapitulations, prepared as posting entries to accounts receivable ledgers for amounts of expense vouchers prepared for employees' travel and related expenses, are to be maintained for a period of 4 years.
- Paid, canceled, and voided checks, other than those issued for the payment of salary and wages, are to be maintained for a period of 4 years.
- Accounts payable records to support disbursements of funds for materials, equipment, supplies, and services, containing originals or copies of the following and related documents: remittance advices and statements, vendors' invoices, invoice audits and distribution slips, receiving and inspection reports or comparable certifications of receipt and inspection of material or services, and debit and credit memoranda, are to be maintained for a period of 4 years.
- Labor cost distribution cards or equivalent documents are to be maintained for a period of 2 years.
- Petty cash records showing a description of expenditures, to whom paid, name of person authorizing payment, and date, including copies of vouchers and other supporting documents, are to be maintained for a period of 2 years.

Pay administration records—FAR Part 4, Subpart 4.705-2

- Payroll sheets, registers, or their equivalent, of salaries and wages paid to individual employees for each payroll period, change slips, and tax withholding statements are to be maintained for a period of 4 years.
- Clock cards or other time and attendance cards are to be maintained for a period of 2 years.
- Paid checks, receipts for wages paid in cash, or other evidence of payments for services rendered by employees are to be maintained for a period of 2 years.

Acquisition and supply records—FAR Part 4, Subpart 4.705-3

- Store requisitions for materials, supplies, equipment, and services are to be maintained for a period of 2 years.
- Work orders for maintenance and other services are to be maintained for a period of 4 years.
- Equipment records, consisting of equipment usage and status reports and equipment repair orders, are to be maintained for a period of 4 years.
- Expendable property records, reflecting accountability for the receipt and use of material in performance of a contract, are to be maintained for a period of 4 years.
- Receiving and inspection report records, consisting of reports reflecting receipt and inspection of supplies, equipment, and materials, are to be maintained for a period of 4 years.
- Purchase order files for supplies, equipment, material, or services used in the performance of a contract, supporting documentation and backup files—including, but not limited to, invoices, and memoranda (such as memoranda of negotiations showing the principal elements of subcontract price)—are to be maintained for a period of 4 years.
- Production records of quality control, reliability, and inspection are to be maintained for a period of 4 years.

2.   How are records maintained?

Records may be maintained in electronic format, provided the electronic records do not contain significant information not shown on the original record copy. Photographic or electronic images of original records are sufficient, provided the following requirements are met:

- The contractor has established procedures to ensure that the imaging process preserves accurate images of the original records, including signatures and other written or graphic images, and that the imaging process is reliable and secure so as to maintain the integrity of the records.
- The contractor maintains an effective indexing system to permit timely and convenient access to the imaged records.
- The contractor retains the original records for a minimum of 1 year after imaging to permit the periodic validation of the imaging systems.

3. How is access to records provided?

The government's expectation is for supporting source detail to be readily available when proposals are submitted to the government, such as those relating to pricing, incurred costs, and termination settlements.

Additional time to provide data may be granted if the data are voluminous, require retrieval from off-site storage, or require preparation of new information/ analyses.

Data not provided timely to the government may be considered a denial of access to contractor records.

Access to records may be provided in a variety of formats from transmittal of paper copies to "SharePoint" sites where data requests, responses, and access is tracked.

SECTION IX
EXPORT CONTROLS AND
NON-DISCLOSURE AGREEMENTS

CONTENTS

Chapter 1

Top Things To Know About U.S. Export Controls

Manik K. Rath and Tamara Jack, LMI

U.S. export controls impose access, dissemination, and participation restrictions on "controlled" information, services, and tangible items. A license or other approval must be obtained from the U.S. government before any controlled item, technical data, or services may be exported. This chapter summarizes key points of the U.S. export controls regime.

1. Who controls what?

- Department of Commerce and Export Administration Regulations (EAR)—most exports of commercial and dual-use commodities, technology, software, and services;
- Department of State and International Traffic in Arms Regulations (ITAR)—exports of defense articles, defense services and technical data; and
- Department of the Treasury, Office of Foreign Assets Control (OFAC)—exports to countries that are targets of broad trade embargoes and economic sanctions that cover more than just exports.

2. What is an export?

A shipment or transmission to a foreign country or disclosure to a foreign person (whether in the United States or abroad) of controlled items, information, or services.

3.   What is a deemed export?

Disclosure (including oral or visual) or transfer of technical data to a foreign person, whether in the United States or abroad, is "deemed" to be an export to the home country or countries of the foreign national. Disclosure to a foreign company in the United States may also be a deemed export.

4.   Who is a foreign person?

Anyone who is not a U.S. citizen, lawful permanent resident (immigrant visa or "green card" holder), or a protected individual (*e.g.*, political asylee).

5.   What is dual use?

Dual-use items are items which are suitable for either military-related use or nonmilitary use. Dual-use items are governed by the EAR.

6.   What is a defense article?

Items specifically designed, developed, configured, adapted, or modified for a military application; also items found on the United States Munitions List within the ITAR.

7.   What is a defense service?

Assistance (including training) in the design, development, engineering, manufacture, production, assembly, testing, repair, maintenance, modification, operation, demilitarization, destruction, processing, or use of defense articles; and furnishing any controlled technical data.

8.   What is controlled defense technical data?

Information, including software, required for the design, development, engineering, production, manufacture, assembly, operation, use, processing, repair, testing, maintenance, or modification of a defense article; any classified information.

9. How do exports occur?

An export can occur by:
- sending or taking a controlled article or data outside the United States or providing it to a foreign person in the United States;
- disclosing (including orally or visually) or transferring technical data to a foreign person in the United States or abroad;
- performing a defense service on behalf of or for the benefit of a foreign person in the United States or abroad;
- escorted tours of company facilities that include controlled articles or data for foreign persons;
- publication of technical data, presentations, and/or technical papers at symposia, conferences or meetings, technical discussions, and even casual conversations.

10. What is an export license or authorization?

An export license, or other authorization such as a Technical Assistance Agreement, represents the government's approval authorizing the export of the controlled item, data, or services for a fixed period of time.

11. When is an export license or authorization required?

If the article or information is governed by the EAR or the ITAR, or the exporter will provide training or defense services in connection with military articles/data to foreign nationals (whether in the United States or abroad), and no regulatory exception applies, a license or authorization must be obtained before any actual or deemed export occurs.

12. When do export controls apply?

The following are examples of situations when export controls apply:

- During foreign national visits;
- During travel to the United States by nationals abroad;
- When publishing in local or international media or presenting at local or international conferences;

- When working with foreign organizations and corporations;
- When working for the U.S. government overseas;
- When assigning work to foreign national employees; and
- Emailing controlled data to foreign persons, whether in the United States or abroad.

13. What is the government approval process and related timing?

The government approval process for export authorizations can be quite lengthy, which makes it critical that company business development personnel provide as much advance notice as possible to the persons responsible for filing export license applications or seeking other export authorizations from the government. The timing and other uncertainties inherent in the government approval process for exports should be reflected in the company's proposals to customers and related contractual commitments.

14. Is the current export control regulatory framework expected to change?

In April 2010, the Obama administration announced its proposal to overhaul the U.S. export control system. The administration's proposal is based on four key principles to achieve this transformation: a single export control list; a single export licensing agency; a single export enforcement coordination agency; and a single coordinated information technology infrastructure. If implemented, this proposal would completely reorganize the current regulatory regime. The administration wants such reforms to be in place in three phases over the course of 2011. However, these changes are likely to be slow in coming. While the first two phases could be accomplished by regulatory changes and executive orders, creating new export control agencies will require congressional action, and Congress remains severely divided over this issue.

Conclusion

This chapter provides an overview of the U.S. export controls regime. A thorough understanding of this complicated area and the associated requirements will ensure that your company is in compliance and successfully operating in this space.

ويو   ويو   ويو

Chapter 2

Non-Disclosure Agreements

Manik K. Rath, Tamara Jack, LMI, and Curtis L. Schehr, DCS

A non-disclosure agreement (NDA) is often one of the first contractual relationships a company has with a prospective business partner. These agreements serve to prohibit the unauthorized disclosure and use of certain information. If a prospective business relationship moves forward, the NDA is sometimes superseded by confidentiality provisions contained in a more definitive transactional agreement.

NDAs are often categorized as either "mutual" or "one-way" and are sometimes referred to as "confidentiality agreements" or by other names. A mutual NDA is one in which each party intends to exchange proprietary and/or confidential information (hereinafter "confidential information") with the other. For example, Company A and Company B may wish to explore the feasibility of entering into a joint venture with each other and would like to better understand each other's technological capabilities, qualifications, and customers. In that circumstance, a mutual, two-way NDA is customary. Conversely, a one-way agreement is used when only one party intends to disclose its confidential information to the other, often the case involving the potential sale or license of a proprietary product or service.

Purpose of an NDA

NDAs serve several purposes, including the following:

- protecting intellectual property,
- demonstrating a commitment to protect company assets, and
- protecting critical business information.

Companies understandably wish to protect the investment they make in technology, personnel, and the inventions, discoveries, processes, improvements, know-how, and other developments they generate for the business. While some intellectual property may obtain protection under patent, trademark, or copyright laws, much intellectual property (including trade secrets) relies on other safeguards for protection. NDAs are an accepted method of obtaining contractual assurances from a third party to whom intellectual property is disclosed that it will not be exploited, used, or shared for any purpose other than that for which the disclosed information is specifically intended.

Second, a company's practice of using NDAs to protect sensitive business information demonstrates to a prospective business partner that the company values its confidential information and is committed to protecting it much like other strategic assets.

Third, NDAs enable a company to safeguard non-public business information such as business plans, marketing strategies, customer information, pricing, and commercial and financial data.

Basic NDA elements

Definition of confidential information
This is clearly a critical element of an NDA and usually contains a laundry list of relevant items, which may include information in oral, written, graphic, electromagnetic or other form, including but not limited to business, financial, and commercial information, prices and pricing methods, marketing and customer information, financial forecasts and projections, technical data and information, trade secrets, methods, processes, know-how, computer programs, products, prototypes, samples, designs, schematics, specifications, and drawings. The agreement should set forth as specifically and comprehensively as possible the scope of information intended to be covered.

Purpose
The agreement should specify the purpose of the NDA and state that the confidential information is only to be disclosed to the other party for that specific, limited purpose. For example, government contractors frequently enter into NDAs the stated purpose of which is to enable the parties to exchange information about their respective capabilities and qualifications to determine their interest in teaming together to pursue a specifically identified federal procurement.

Identifying confidential information

NDAs should describe the method by which information is to be designated as confidential information and therefore subject to the restrictions and other provisions of the NDA. While some NDAs will not require that information needs to be marked in order to be entitled to confidential treatment, the more customary practice is to require all tangible confidential information to be marked "CONFIDENTIAL" or bear a similar conspicuous legend.

Confidential information disclosed orally presents its own unique challenges and is typically addressed in one of two ways: one approach is to require that, within a specified period of time (e.g., 10 days after the verbal disclosure), the disclosing party identify in writing to the receiving party the fact and content of the verbal disclosure. The second approach, which is more pragmatic though legally less desirable, is to require the disclosing party to inform the receiving party orally prior to disclosure that the information to be disclosed is confidential information.

Exclusions

NDAs should define the information that will be not subject to the provisions of the NDA. These exclusions typically involve information: (i) already known to the receiving party prior to disclosure; (ii) independently developed by the receiving party and appropriately evidenced; (iii) in the public domain other than as a result of a breach of the NDA by the disclosing party; and (iv) received by the receiving party from another source having no obligation to the disclosing party.

No promises or commitments

Parties to an NDA typically include a provision stating that neither the execution of the NDA nor the exchange of confidential information should give rise to any commitment or promise to buy, sell, or enter into any kind of business relationship. This provision protects both parties and can prove important if the relationship turns sour and either party is inclined to assert that it's "owed" something more.

Treatment of confidential information post-termination

This topic is sometimes the subject of negotiation revolving around (i) whether the receiving party may keep one copy for archival purposes in case of litigation; and (ii) whether the confidential information must be returned to the disclosing party, or alternatively may be destroyed with an accompanying certification to that effect. The issue of retaining a copy of the confidential information for archival purposes is usually determined as a function of the parties' relative bargaining position.

Destruction of confidential information is certainly preferable from the standpoint of the receiving party and is often successfully negotiated into the NDA.

Term of NDA and non-disclosure obligations

The two time elements of an NDA are (i) the term during which the parties may exchange confidential information that will be subject to the NDA; and (ii) the period of non-disclosure and non-use. The first time element varies from agreement to agreement, but is typically a term of 1 to 3 years. Second, the confidentiality period is most always a key item of negotiation and varies from several years from the date of disclosure to an indefinite period.

Other provisions

Other principal terms contained in an NDA include such matters as remedies for breach, governing law, jurisdiction and venue, and assignment.

Conclusion

The negotiation and execution of an NDA is a baby-step in the development of a potential business relationship that could substantively support your company's growth. As a practical matter, the NDA is simply a door-opener that enables the parties to explore the feasibility and level of interest in working together on matters of potentially mutually benefit. While a company's business people are understandably anxious to begin discussions with the other firm, they should be informed by the company's executives or legal counsel of the perils of doing so before the NDA is in place. At the same time, however, the company's legal counsel needs to stay focused on the truly important elements of the NDA and avoid getting caught up in non-productive negotiations over immaterial provisions of the agreement. No one wants to have a potentially fruitful relationship scuttled over an NDA negotiation impasse, unless of course, the difficulties (and/or personalities) encountered suggest that more substantive downstream dealings with the other party could be even more divisive.

SECTION X
RISK INSURANCE AND EMPLOYEE BENEFITS

CONTENTS

Chapter 1

Fundamentals of Business Insurance

David L. Schaefer, AH&T Insurance

Securing a well-constructed property and casualty (business) insurance program is one of the fundamental steps of establishing and maintaining business operations. There are a variety of statutory, contractual, and business purposes for coverage that may influence the types and limits of insurance required or desired to meet the needs of the business and protect the organization from unforeseen losses that could potentially destroy or harm it financially.

Business insurance can allow an organization to perform the following key elements of business compliance and enablement:

- Comply with the law
- Comply with and facilitate execution of leases and other contracts
- Securitize loans and protect assets/equity
- Attract and retain a high-quality board of directors and key employees
- Secure contracts with customers and partners
- Protect income stream and employees
- Transfer liability and costs of defense from the organization's balance sheet to insurers.

1. Statutory insurance requirements

The Commonwealth of Virginia requires any individual or organization with three or more employees to purchase workers compensation insurance. All other states and the District of Columbia have similar requirements. Even if the insurance coverage is not purchased, costs (medical and lost time) stemming from injury or accidents on the job to employees or uninsured subcontractors are mandated to be covered by the employing organization or individual.

Virginia also mandates a minimum amount of <u>automobile liability insurance</u> for autos owned and operated by anyone, with the exception of certain types of "farm use" vehicles. Every state in the United States has similar requirements that vary by jurisdiction.

The United States requires that organizations with qualified retirement plan(s) under the Employee Retirement Income Security Act (ERISA) maintain a bond (<u>ERISA Bond</u>) to protect assets of the plan(s).

<u>Defense Base Act (DBA) insurance</u> is required by the U.S. government for virtually any overseas work on a specific government contract. Like workers' compensation, DBA covers a portion of employees' medical and disability expenses for injuries and accidents that occur arising out of their employment but the benefit levels are normally higher than state mandated coverages and there are special provisions for acts of war.

Certain states mandate that <u>supplemental disability insurance</u> is secured for employees working in that jurisdiction. Fines and penalties may be assessed by the state for organizations failing to provide the coverage, or in certain cases, evidence of the coverage to the responsible governing organization in the state.

2. Contractual insurance requirements

Many organizations first secure basic property and liability insurance when required to do so by a lease for office, warehouse, or other real estate space. Most leases contain a variety of insurance requirements that an organization must typically satisfy by providing to the landlord or property management company evidence of coverage in the form of a <u>certificate of insurance</u> prior to occupying the leased space. The most common types of insurance coverage required by a lease include:

- Property insurance for the contents owned by the tenant or for which they are responsible; and frequently the value of the betterments and improvements (floor coverings, walls other than exterior or load-bearing, wall coverings, ceilings, lighting, etc.) to the space being occupied. Sometimes the landlord will also require business interruption insurance to cover the tenant's lost income in case an insured loss negatively impacts the tenant's ability to pay rent;
- Commercial general liability insurance for liability arising out of bodily injury or property damage associated with business operations or products/ services—often with specific terms and limits dictated by the contract;
- Workers' compensation insurance to cover injuries or accidents to employees arising from their employment or engagement;
- Automobile liability insurance if vehicles owned, leased, or used for the benefit of the tenant will be operated in any parking facility associated with the leased premises.

Contracts for services and/or products are also a major source of insurance requirements imposed by a customer or other third parties. Many of these agreements include some, most, or all of the insurance provisions covered by leases. Frequently, these agreements go further, with requirements for additional coverage limits and other types of insurance not required by most leases. Some typical insurance provisions contained in contracts include:

- Professional liability (E&O) insurance provides for liability and legal defense expenses arising out of the organization's professional services and the consequential financial harm it may cause the customer and third parties. For example, an IT system is provided that does not perform as intended, and the customer loses money and customers as a result of the poor performance of the system.
- International coverages. Many insurance policies purchased in the United STates have specific provisions setting forth the territorial limits (e.g., the United States) to which the coverage may apply. If the work under the contract extends beyond the territorial limits of the policy, the coverage must be broadened or additional policies secured to satisfy the contractually mandated insurance requirements.

3. Other insurance coverages frequently purchased for business purposes

Directors & officers liability insurance (D&O) provides a funding mechanism for the indemnity obligation (and associated defense expenses) most organizations have to their board of directors and officers for the personal liability that may arise from decisions made on behalf of the company.

Employment practices liability insurance (EPL) provides coverage for liability associated with the management of employees—specifically in the areas of wrongful termination, harassment and discrimination.

Fiduciary liability insurance—Similar to D&O insurance, plan fiduciaries have personal liability for decisions that are made in the name of the administration of ERISA qualified plans. Fiduciary liability insurance can cover defense and indemnity obligations the company may have to those employees that serve in a fiduciary capacity for the company's retirement plans.

Umbrella/excess liability insurance provides additional insurance capacity for certain types of liability insurance coverage. Typically, umbrella liability coverage will extend limits of protection for commercial general liability, employer's liability, and automobile liability insurance coverage.

Property in transit coverages can provide insurance coverage for property the insured owns or is responsible for which may not stay at a fixed insured location.

The comments in this summary are necessarily brief and do not attempt to be comprehensive in scope. Insurance coverage is always governed by the specific language of the applicable policy(s). It is recommended that a reputable insurance broker and a qualified attorney be consulted when securing insurance coverage.

Chapter 2

Contract Risk Management, Insurance, and Compliance

By David L. Schaefer, AH&T Insurance[6]

Utilizing sound risk transfer strategies is a key element of risk management allowing organizations to prosper and grow without assuming unnecessary risks. Managing risk through contracts is a fundamental element of this process. Insurance underwriters who service technology companies and company personnel carefully review contract terms and conditions under which companies operate to secure work and maximize protection from liability. Sound strategies in this arena can make a big difference in the risk an organization faces from its work and in the availability and cost of various forms of insurance.

1. Contractual provisions

A business should know how contractual provisions can open up—or limit—the company's exposure to various liabilities. When a customer disputes or complains about the use of your products or services, the contract you entered into with that customer is your principal line of defense. Described below are some of the many contractual provisions that may help limit your company's liability exposures to customers and third parties.

Limitations of liability
You should employ clear language tailored to your industry that minimizes your exposure to consequential, punitive, special, and similar damages and ensures

---

[6]   The author gratefully acknowledges the assistance of Arnold Morse, General Counsel to CACI International, in preparing this chapter.

that the company's maximum liability is limited to the price of the contract or service provided to the customer.

Indemnification

Help protect your assets by including indemnification wording that inures to your benefit—rather than leaving indemnity as a matter subject to interpretation. Indemnity is a voluntary obligation to compensate another party to a contract for any loss that such other party may suffer during the performance of the contract. Wherever possible, your contracts should stipulate the indemnification procedures, terms, and conditions that will apply in the event of a dispute. If both parties to a contract agree to specific indemnity obligations, this can be treated as an advance agreement under which each party agrees to compensate the other for liability and losses arising out of certain acts, omissions, or events for the value of a failure before one occurs, rather than trying to sort out the value for a loss after it has happened.

Amendments and modifications

Procedures required to make binding amendments and modifications to your contracts should be clearly outlined. The severity of a potential claim may be better managed if changes to product and service delivery schedules and specifications are carefully documented. Undocumented changes can become contentious issues leading to litigation.

Performance obligations

Be as realistic as possible in your proposals, avoiding promises of lofty performance standards. If you enter into contracts with incomplete specifications, you may very well expose your firm to potential claims and litigation. Contract performance obligations and relevant acceptance criteria should always be detailed in the contracts your firm executes.

Disclaiming warranties

Make sure warranty disclaimers are included in the proposal and resulting contract, if appropriate. They may help minimize your litigation exposure by identifying the types and scope of warranties you are willing to offer. These disclaimers should conform to the requirements of the Uniform Commercial Code for type style and content.

2. Liability and insurance "flow-down"

Liability and insurance "flow-down" provisions are also very important. If your work for a customer includes the use of products or work by third parties and/

or subcontractors, it is vitally important to impose upon them as many of the conditions of the contract your organization enters into with the customer as possible. Secure indemnification and appropriate representations from your subcontractors that they have adequate insurance coverage to fund defense, settlement or judgment expenses for your benefit for the types of losses for which they may be wholly or partially responsible. Some typical insurance conditions to require from third parties and subcontractors:

- Statutory workers' compensation, employer's liability and supplemental disability insurance—as required by the jurisdictions where the work takes place.
- Commercial general liability (CGL) insurance, including products and completed operations coverage.
- Errors and omissions liability insurance if the product or service from your supplier can cause financial harm without causing tangible damage to persons or property.
- Automobile liability insurance if your sub-contractor will be driving in the course of the work being performed for your organization.
- Property insurance if the individual or organization working on your behalf has responsibility (care, custody, or control) for property that is yours or will become part of the deliverable to your customer or other third party.

When making the provisioning of insurance part of an agreement, it is important to always require a certificate of insurance from your supplier or subcontractor as a means of verifying their compliance with those terms and conditions of the contract. In most instances, requiring the subcontractor's insurance coverages to be "primary and non-contributory" as it relates to their work under the contract will further insulate your organization and its insurance program from losses caused by a subcontractor. Insurance policies typically renew annually, and you should require a new certificate of insurance every time your subcontractor's policies renew until your subcontracts with them are complete, and possibly longer if liability stemming from a project could continue post-completion.

Requiring and reviewing your subcontractors' certificates of insurance is a time-consuming but critical task that is well worth the protection and potential savings to your organization. If the number of subcontractors and vendors is more than your company's internal resources are able to manage, there are services that automate the process and can even help with the interpretation of just what these documents are evidencing.

The comments in this summary are necessarily brief and do not attempt to be comprehensive in scope. Insurance coverage is always governed by the specific language of the applicable policy(s). It is recommended that a reputable insurance broker and a qualified attorney be consulted when securing needed insurance coverage.

Chapter 3

Common and Costly Employee Benefits and HR Mistakes

Brent D'Agostino, AH&T Insurance

Mistakes in human resources and employee benefits cost an employer real money—extra benefits, complaints, lawsuits, government-assessed fines and penalties, and attorney fees, to name a few. This chapter outlines several lessons learned that will help you avoid costly mistakes.

1. Not timely depositing employee contributions into employee benefit plan.

Employers sometimes wait too long to deposit salary deferrals into a qualified retirement plan, such as a 401(k) plan. Salary deferrals become plan assets as soon as the contributions can be reasonably segregated from the employer's general assets. According to the Department of Labor (DOL), such deposits should be made by employers no later than the 15th business day of the following month. This is an outside guideline, and deposits should be made sooner. If deposits are not timely made, the DOL and IRS may levy fines, penalties, and retroactive earnings for late contributions. The deposit rule for elective deferrals applies to all types of participant contributions, including special deferrals (such as catch-up), after-tax contributions, and loan repayments.

Solution: Deposit employee contributions as soon as reasonably possible following issuance of the paycheck from which the contribution was withheld—generally at the same time as other contributions are made but not more than 7 to 10 days from the date of issuance of the paycheck.

2. Not making matching and profit-sharing contributions on a timely basis.

Many employers make the mistake of not making matching and profit-sharing contributions on a timely basis. If your employee benefit plan provides for matching and profit-sharing contributions, the deadline for making these contributions and depositing them into the plan's trust is determined first by reviewing the plan document, which may contain deadlines.

If the plan document requires contributions be made by the date required by law, then the deadline generally will be determined by Internal Revenue Code section 404(a), which requires that matching and profit-sharing contributions be made before the due date of the plan sponsor's tax return, including extensions. Tax exempt employers must make and deposit contributions by the 15th day of the 6th month following the close of a plan year. Plan documents may require depositing matching and profit-sharing contributions sooner, which is likely the case with matching contributions that are calculated on a payroll-by-payroll basis and deposited sooner by plan design. The same penalties as above apply.

Solution: Read your plan documents and understand when matching contributions must be made.

3. Incorrectly computing matching contributions.

A typical plan matching contribution provision states that an employer will pay 50 cents for each $1 an employee contributes to the plan on a pre-tax basis up to 6 percent of compensation, which results in a maximum employer contribution of 3 percent of compensation. It is most common for plan administrators and payroll systems to calculate matching contributions on a weekly payroll-by-payroll basis.

If an employee earning $60,000 a year makes the 6 percent contribution throughout the year on a payroll-by-payroll basis, the employee will contribute $3,600 to the plan, and the employer will provide a matching contribution equal to $1,800. Assume another employee earning the same base salary contributes 12 percent for 6 months. This employee has also contributed a total of $3,600 to the plan, but will only receive a $900 employer match. This occurs because the employer only matches on the first 6 percent of pay when a deferral is made. In the first 6 months, the employees would receive his maximum per pay employer contribution. However in the last 6 months, no employee deferrals occur because the employee has "maxed out." Because there is no employee deferral, there is nothing for the employer to match on these payroll periods.

This same scenario also often occurs with executives who receive large bonuses early in the year and request the maximum contribution be withheld from the bonus.

Solution: Employers that provide "make-up" contributions at the end of the year are able to ensure that employees making the same annual employee savings contributions receive the same matching contributions. If employers are using a prototype plan, make-up contributions may not be a viable option. In this case, educating employees on the implications of changing deferral elections and limits is important. Also, if matching contributions are not calculated correctly or in accordance with the plan document, the IRS's Employee Plan Compliance Resolution System Program allows employers to correct errors with leniency at any time before they are identified by audit.

4.   Late enrollment of employees in employee benefit plans.

Employers often fail to timely enroll employees in tax-qualified retirement plans, and sometimes try to exclude part-time employees from participation. A tax-qualified plan may exclude an employee based on age (up to 21) or service (generally up to 1 year of service in which he/she is credited with at least 1,000 hours of service), but not based on part-time status.

If you wrongfully exclude employees, the DOL and the IRS can levy retroactive employer contributions, elective deferrals, and earnings for employees that were wrongfully excluded. The IRS-approved correction for failing to allow an employee to make an elective deferral for part of a plan year is to make an employer contribution equal to 50 percent of the "average deferral percentage" of the employee's group (either highly or non-highly compensated), multiplied by the employee's compensation for that part of the year.

Former employees who are rehired and who had completed the plan's eligibility requirements before terminating are eligible to begin participating immediately upon rehire.

<u>Solution:</u> Include in the retirement plan a requirement that all eligible employees work at least 1,000 hours in a 12-month period (unless such employees are excluded based on a "service-neutral" classification).

Chapter 4

Do Government Contractors Have Special Risk Management and Insurance Needs?

David L. Schaefer, AH&T Insurance[7]

Doing business with the U.S. government is different from the commercial environment, and while your company's exposure to loss in some areas may be limited, contracting with the federal government increases your risk in others. This chapter outlines some of the reasons that government contractors should give special attention to insurance and risk management issues.

- The Federal Acquisition Regulation (FAR) and Department of Defense FAR Supplement (DFAR) contain numerous clauses that make a contractor responsible for *government-furnished equipment, property, or motor vehicles* when the contractor is in possession of or using those items. Conversely, the FAR/DFAR also offer a government contractor relief from responsibility for damage to these items if certain clauses are included in the contract.

- The FAR/DFAR also offer some protection from certain product and professional liability suits. From an underwriter's perspective, *many products and services developed by a government contractor are high risk*, especially if the contractor cannot share the government's sovereign immunity. The art of products and professional liability underwriting is understanding to what degree, if any, the prime contractor and its subcontractors can face liability suits from third parties.

---

[7]   The author gratefully acknowledges the assistance of Michele Cappello, General Counsel to NCI Information Systems, Inc., in preparing this chapter.

- Many government contracting officers do not fully understand or appreciate how a particular contract's wording can affect the _contractor's ability to obtain insurance_ at a reasonable cost. Anticipating problems and educating contracting officers on insurance underwriting considerations can solve many problems before they mushroom into a costly result.
- Much of the products and professional liability underwriting standards used in the insurance industry revolve around the contract used by insureds with their customers. Government prime contractors usually do not have the luxury of using their own contracts and have to accept _standard government contract terms_ based upon the FAR/DFAR and other provisions required by the federal government. Understanding contract risk management techniques, especially if you are using your customer's proposed contract, is key to limiting the likelihood and severity of a loss or damages (as noted below, the government usually does not sue its prime contractors).
- Although the federal government usually does not sue its contractors for products and professional liability, it has the _right to terminate for default, terminate for convenience, delay payments, or suspend the award of further contracts_ to the prime contractor. In other words, the government still carries a big stick with potentially significant financial implications for the prime contractor. Therefore, understanding and keeping the customer satisfied is just as valid for a prime contractor as it is for a company selling to commercial customers. Government contracts such as indefinite delivery/indefinite quantity contracts may be structured and administered by the customer such that the contractor does not know if it will have certain exposures until the government awards task orders under the contract and, even then, may not be able to quantify the exposure. Telling an insurance underwriter "I may need Defense Base Act coverage but I'm not sure if we'll be sending anyone overseas," or "I don't know yet if we'll be responsible for storing hazardous chemicals," can lead to higher premiums or a lack of interest by underwriters without a knowledgeable broker explaining the realities of government contracting to those underwriters. An insurance broker who is a government contracts risk specialist should be able to guide you and manage communications with the underwriter so they understand your current levels of exposure to loss and potential near-term needs.
- Contracting with the federal government can mean _unusual exposures to loss_ such as civilian employees on military equipment or vessels; in high-hazard environments such as Afghanistan or Iraq; or working at

government facilities with unusual risks. Workers' compensation or DBA coverage in these situations must be properly obtained to protect the prime contractor.

- Even though your end customer is a federal government agency, you may have commercial subcontractors or be a subcontractor yourself. Although the contract may be largely governed by the FAR, the _relationship between prime contractor and subcontractor_ also has commercial and common law elements.

- Failure to deliver a working product on time that results in another contractor losing payments from the federal agency customer can result in a _products or professional liability claim_.

- Understanding the legal theories and background of the government contractor defense and similar provisions such as the product liability immunity contained in the _Homeland Security SAFETY Act_ are critical to securing robust and cost effective products liability insurance coverages.

The comments in this summary are necessarily brief and do not attempt to be comprehensive in scope. Insurance coverage is always governed by the specific language of the applicable policy(s). It is recommended that a reputable insurance broker and a qualified attorney be consulted when securing needed insurance coverage.

Notes

Chapter 5

Retirement Plan Compliance— A Fiduciary Checklist

James E. Maulfair, AH&T Insurance[8]

Overview

Small business owners want to be competitive in the marketplace. This typically includes the need to sponsor a "qualified" retirement plan—such as a profit sharing or a 401(k) plan—to provide a retirement savings benefit for the company's executives and employees. The Employee Retirement Income Savings Act of 1974 (ERISA) governs these plans.

It is imperative that small businesses take their fiduciary responsibilities seriously, as any breach can mean personal liability that the IRS and DOL may impose. Small businesses often do not have the staff to adequately monitor and evaluate the performance of the retirement plan and the plan providers regarding ERISA compliance, recordkeeping, and investment management. These tasks may fall on benefit brokers, financial advisors, and third-party administrators (TPAs), who sometimes have little or no fiduciary liability compared with the employer and those handling the day to day operations of the plan. The fiduciary compliance checklist provided below is a general guideline designed to assist small business owners on what to look for from their plan and questions they should ask their plan providers to maximize plan performance.

---

[8] The author gratefully acknowledges the assistance of Jewell Esposito, Esq., Chamberlain Hrdlicka, in preparing this chapter.

Basic fiduciary compliance checklist

1. Review the definitions of "employee" and "eligibility" in your plan document and confirm that you are providing all eligible employees enrollment materials to enter the plan.
2. Follow the plan definition of pay for deferral, matching, and discretionary contribution purposes.
3. If you have a custom plan document, consider filing for a favorable determination letter. The determination letter is documentation that the plan design has been reviewed the IRS and deemed to be a qualified plan under IRC Section 401 (a). In any subsequent submission to the IRS, you would have to provide it with a copy of the determination letter.
4. Submit plan contributions to the TPA or plan trustee as applicable within 2-3 days after payroll deductions are made, or the soonest possible date thereafter. Report any purchase or sale of any part of your company (sale of stock or assets) to your TPA, plan trustee, or other plan advisor.
5. Report any layoff of 15 percent or more of your employees to your TPA, plan trustee, or other plan advisor. Obtain an independent plan auditor if you have more than 100-120 employees, as your plan may require an outside ERISA plan audit.
6. If you have not updated your summary plan description (SPD) in the last 5 years, or since the last time you made changes to the plan design, contact your plan provider and advisor.
7. Document and retain minutes for any plan review and retirement plan related meetings held by the company.
8. With respect to a 401(k) plan, if you have not already completed and executed your investment and ERISA 404(c) policy statements, do so immediately with the help of a financial advisor.
9. Follow the guidelines of your investment due diligence reviews. If you need to add, delete, or freeze funds based on the research and analysis presented in such reviews, do so! Remember that "no action" by a plan fiduciary is a form of "action" from the perspective of the DOL.
10. Lower your overall plan administration costs by forcing IRA rollovers for terminated participants' account balances of $1,000-$5,000.
11. Work with the plan provider to take "reasonable steps" to locate plan participants who have terminated employment.
12. Make sure that summary annual reports are distributed within 9 months after the end of the plan year.

13. If applicable, make sure that the summary of material modifications is distributed within 210 days after the end of the plan year.
14. Remember that you may not be allowed to exclude your part-time employees from participating in the plan. If you are attempting to legitimately exclude a class of employees, confer with your plan provider on how to properly do so.
15. Consider having plan forfeitures first to pay plan expenses and then to offset the cost of employer matching or discretionary contributions.
16. Ensure that the service you are getting from your broker, financial advisor, and TPA is competitive and reasonable. Conduct and document the results of your periodic review.
17. Have your broker, financial advisor, or TPA run scenarios to show you less expensive ways to administer your plan.
18. Visit the IRS and DOL government websites to review the most commonly occurring retirement plan mistakes. Perform a self-audit to ensure that you are not encountering these problems, prior to the IRS or DOL finding these mistakes.
19. Evaluate the extent and amount of fiduciary bond and fiduciary liability coverage you must purchase. Note that the bond and the coverage are two different products. One covers the retirement plan; the other, the fiduciary personally.

Notes

Chapter 6

COBRA Overview

Brent D'Agostino, AH&T Insurance

COBRA premium reduction

The American Recovery and Reinvestment Act of 2009 (ARRA), as amended on December 19, 2009, by the Department of Defense Appropriations Act, 2010, provides for premium reductions for health benefits under the Consolidated Omnibus Budget Reconciliation Act of 1985, commonly called COBRA. Eligible individuals pay only 35 percent of their COBRA premiums, and the remaining 65 percent is reimbursed to the coverage provider through a tax credit. To qualify, individuals must experience a COBRA qualifying event—that is, the involuntary termination of a covered employee's employment. The involuntary termination must occur during the period that began September 1, 2008, and ended on May 31, 2010. The premium reduction applies to periods of health coverage that began on or after February 17, 2009, and lasts for up to 15 months.

What is COBRA?

COBRA gives workers and their families who lose their health benefits the right to purchase group health coverage provided by the plan under certain circumstances.

If the employer continues to offer a group health plan, the employee and his/her family can retain their group health coverage for up to 18 months by paying group rates. The COBRA premium may be higher than what the individual was paying while employed, but generally the cost is lower than that for private, individual health insurance coverage.

The plan administrator must notify affected employees of their right to elect COBRA. The employee and his/her family each have 60 days to elect COBRA coverage; otherwise, they lose all rights to COBRA benefits.

COBRA generally does not apply to plans sponsored by employers with fewer than 20 employees. Many states have similar requirements for insurance companies that provide coverage to small employers. The premium reduction is available for insurers covered by these state laws.

Changes to COBRA in the 2010 DOD Act

The 2010 DOD act extended the COBRA premium reduction eligibility period for 2 months until May 31, 2010, and increased the maximum period for receiving the subsidy for an additional 6 months (from 9 to 15 months). It is very likely that Congress will continue this approach—a series of short-term fixes, rather than a longer extension—for the remainder of the year.

In addition, individuals who had reached the end of the reduced premium period before the legislation extended it to 15 months will have an extension of their grace period to pay the reduced premium. To continue their coverage, they must pay the 35 percent of premium costs by 30 days after notice of the extension is provided by their plan administrator.

Eligibility for the premium reduction

The premium reduction for COBRA continuation coverage is available to "assistance eligible individuals." An "assistance eligible individual" is the employee or a member of his/her family who:
* has a qualifying event for continuation coverage under COBRA or a state law that provides comparable continuation coverage (for example, so-called "mini-COBRA" laws)—that is, the employee's involuntary termination at any point from September 1, 2008, through February 28, 2010; and
* elects COBRA coverage.

Those who are eligible for other group health coverage (such as a spouse's plan) or Medicare are not eligible for the premium reduction. There is no premium reduction for premiums paid for periods of coverage that began prior to February 17, 2009.

Assistance eligible individuals (AEIs) who pay 35 percent of their COBRA premiums are treated as having paid the full amount. The premium reduction (65 percent of the full premium) is reimbursable to the employer, insurer, or health plan as a credit against certain employment taxes.

Income limits

If an individual's modified adjusted gross income for the tax year in which the premium assistance is received exceeds $145,000 (or $290,000 for joint filers), then the amount of the premium reduction during the tax year must be repaid. For taxpayers with adjusted gross income between $125,000 and $145,000 (or $250,000 and $290,000, for joint filers), the amount of the premium reduction that must be repaid is reduced proportionately. Individuals may permanently waive the right to premium reduction, but may not later obtain the premium reduction if their adjusted gross incomes end up below the limits. If you think that your income may exceed the amounts above, consult your tax preparer or contact the IRS at www.irs.gov.

Period of coverage

The premium reduction applies to periods of coverage beginning on or after February 17, 2009. A period of coverage is a month or shorter period for which the plan charges a COBRA premium. The premium reduction for an individual ends upon eligibility for other group coverage (or Medicare), after 15 months of the reduction, or when the maximum period of COBRA coverage ends, whichever occurs first. Individuals paying reduced COBRA premiums must inform their plans if they become eligible for coverage under another group health plan or Medicare.

Notice requirements

Even though the subsidy is available only to involuntarily terminated workers, some revised COBRA notice requirements apply more broadly to all qualified beneficiaries. On March 19, 2009, the DOL released model notices that employers may use to notify COBRA qualified beneficiaries of the new COBRA subsidy. The DOL has made available four different notification forms, along with application forms for COBRA qualified beneficiaries to complete and return to obtain a subsidized COBRA premium.

All of the model notices provide a space for the employee to attest to the fact that he or she was involuntarily terminated. There is also a space for the employer to indicate, upon receipt of the election form, whether the employee's application for treatment as an AEI has been approved or denied. If an application is denied, the employee may appeal the decision to either the DOL or the Department of Health and Human Services. The Departments are required to make a determination regarding the appeal within 15 business days.

Expedited review of denials of premium reduction

Individuals who are denied treatment as AEIs s and thus are denied eligibility for the premium reduction (whether by their plan, employer, or insurer) may request an expedited review of the denial by the U.S. Department of Labor. The department must make a determination within 15 business days of receipt of a completed request for review. The official application form is available at www. dol.gov/COBRA and can be filed online or submitted by fax or mail.

Chapter 7

Election Changes Within a Cafeteria Plan

Brent D'Agostino, AH&T Insurance

This chapter provides a high-level overview of the IRS regulations relating to permitted election changes made to an employer's cafeteria plan. A cafeteria plan is a written plan that complies with applicable provisions of the Internal Revenue Code. They are sometimes called Section 125 plans or flexible benefit plans. Cafeteria plans allow employers to offer employees the choice between at least one qualified taxable benefit, typically cash compensation, and one or more qualified nontaxable benefits, such as accident and health coverage. The term "cafeteria plans" derives from the fact that employees are free to choose their benefits from a menu of options. The applicable regulations may be found at 26 CFR § 1.125-4 and in proposed regulations published in August 2007. The proposed regulations may be relied upon for guidance until final regulations are adopted and released.

Elections and election changes in general

Under a cafeteria plan, elections must be made by employees before the first day of the plan year or the date taxable benefits would currently be available, whichever comes first. Participant elections generally must be irrevocable until the beginning of the next plan year. Employers do not have to permit any exceptions to this rule. However, an employer may design its cafeteria plan to permit an employee to change his or her election during the year if the participant experiences a "change in status," an event for which the IRS allows a participant to make a change in election that is consistent with the event. The IRS regulations list the permitted election change events which may support a mid-year election change.

Described below are events cafeteria plans may recognize as entitling a plan participant to change his or her elections (if the change is consistent with the event). An employer's cafeteria plan may not be more generous than the IRS permits and in fact may limit to a greater extent than the IRS the election change events it will recognize.

If a cafeteria plan incorporates one or more of the change in status rules, an employee who experiences a change in status is permitted to revoke an existing election and make a new election consistent with the event for the remaining portion of the applicable plan year, but only with respect to cash or other taxable benefits that are not yet currently available. Only an employee of the employer sponsoring a cafeteria plan is authorized to make, revoke or change elections in the employer's cafeteria plan. Neither the employee's spouse, dependent nor any other individual other than the employee may make, revoke or change elections under the plan. Changes may be made by employees using electronic means, such as via the internet.

Permitted election change events

Cafeteria plans may recognize the following events as entitling an employee to make election changes during a plan year:

1. *Change in status*
The IRS considers the following events to be changes in status if they affect eligibility for coverage under an employer's plan:

- Change in employee's legal marital status (including marriage, death of spouse, divorce, legal separation, and annulment),
- Change in number of dependents (including birth, death, adoption, and placement for adoption),
- Change in employment status of employee, employee's spouse, or employee's dependent (including termination or commencement of employment, commencement of or return from an unpaid leave of absence, and a change in worksite),
- Dependent's satisfying or ceasing to satisfy dependent eligibility requirements (including attainment of age, student status, or any similar circumstance),
- Change in place of residence of the employee, spouse, or dependent, and
- Commencement or termination of adoption proceedings, for purposes of adoption assistance provided through a cafeteria plan.

2. Cost changes

If the cost of a plan increases or decreases during a coverage period, and under the terms of the plan, employees are required to make a corresponding change in their payments, the cafeteria plan may on a reasonable and consistent basis, automatically make a prospective increase or decrease in affected employees' elective contributions for the plan.

3. Significant cost changes

If the cost charged to an employee for a benefit package option significantly increases or significantly decreases during a period, the cafeteria plan may permit the employee to make a corresponding election change under the cafeteria plan.

4. Significant curtailment of coverage

If an employee or an employee's spouse or dependent has a significant curtailment of coverage under a plan during a coverage period, the plan may permit the employee to revoke his or her election for that coverage and to elect other coverage on a prospective basis under another benefit option providing similar coverage is available.

5. Addition or improvement of benefit package option

If, during a coverage period, a plan adds a new benefit package option or other coverage option, or if coverage under an existing benefit package option or other coverage option is significantly improved, the cafeteria plan may permit eligible employees to revoke their elections under the cafeteria plan and make an election on a prospective basis for coverage under the new or improved benefit package option.

6. Change in coverage of spouse or dependent under another employer plan

A cafeteria plan may permit an employee to make a prospective election change that is on account of and corresponds with a change made under another employer's plan if the other plan allows an election change that is permissible under the IRS regulations, or when the other employer plan has a different period of coverage. Employees generally can change their elections for accident and health coverage and group-term life insurance when they:

- experience certain changes in their marital status, numbers of dependents, employment, or residence;
- opt for special enrollment rights under the federal Health Insurance Portability and Accountability Act;

- are ordered to change coverage for their dependents by a court in divorce, legal separation, annulment, or change-in-legal-custody proceedings;
- become eligible or ineligible for Medicare or Medicaid;
- take leave under the federal Family and Medical Leave Act; and
- experience significant cost or coverage changes under your cafeteria plan.

7. Loss of certain other health coverage

A cafeteria plan may permit an employee to make an election on a prospective basis to add coverage under a cafeteria plan for the employee, spouse, or dependent if they lose coverage under any group health coverage sponsored by a governmental or educational institution. This includes coverage under a State Children's Health Insurance Program (SCHIP).

8. Changes in 401(k) contributions

A cafeteria plan may permit an employee to modify or revoke elections related to a 401(k) plan in accordance with Internal Revenue Code sections 401(k) and (m).

9. HIPAA special enrollment rights

A cafeteria plan may permit an employee to revoke an election for coverage under a group health plan during a period of coverage and make a new election that corresponds with the special enrollment rights provided under HIPAA.

10. COBRA Qualifying Event.

A cafeteria plan may permit the employee to elect to increase payments under the employer's cafeteria plan in order to pay for the continuation coverage for which an employee, spouse, or dependent has become eligible.

11. Judgments, decrees, or orders

A cafeteria plan may change the employee's election to provide coverage for a child if a judgment, decree, or order requires coverage for the child under the employee's plan, or permit the employee to cancel coverage for the child if an order requires another individual to cover the child.

12. Entitlement to Medicare or Medicaid

If an employee, spouse, or dependent becomes entitled to coverage under Medicare or Medicaid or loses such entitlement, the cafeteria plan may permit the employee to make a prospective election change to cancel/reduce or reinstate/ increase coverage under the accident or health plan.

13. Family Medical Leave Act (FMLA) leave

An employee taking leave under the federal FMLA may revoke an existing election of accident or health plan coverage and make such other election for the remaining portion of the period of coverage as may be provided for under the FMLA.

14. Pre-tax health savings account (HSA) contributions

If HSA contributions are made through salary reduction under a cafeteria plan, employees may prospectively elect, revoke, or change salary reduction elections for HSA contributions at any time during the plan year with respect to salary that has not been earned at the time of the election.

A cafeteria plan that intends to recognize one or more election change events provided for in the regulations should review its plan document before making any change in plan administration. Unless the plan document states that it will follow any guidance provided in temporary, final, or proposed IRS regulations, a formal written plan amendment is recommended in order to properly authorize the plan administrator to recognize and act upon such change events.

Notes

SECTION XI
CORPORATE GOVERNANCE

CONTENTS

Chapter 1

Overview

David J. Charles, Pillsbury Winthrop Shaw Pittman LLP, and Michele R. Cappello, NCI Information Systems, Inc.

1. Introduction

The issues regarding governance of a business entity depend on the form of the entity in question and the jurisdiction under which it is organized. Corporations, limited liability companies (LLCs), and partnerships are all creatures of state law. The applicable state law provides the basic framework for how each such entity must be organized and function. A business entity must comply with the governance requirements of applicable state law in order to ensure that it receives the full benefit of the rights, privileges and protections thereunder (most importantly, limitations on liability of owners, directors/managers, and officers, in case of corporations and LLCs). This chapter outlines the fundamental formation and governance requirements for corporations and LLCs under Virginia law and Delaware law.

2. Applicable law

Corporations
The Virginia Stock Corporation Act, Title 13.1, Chapter 9 of the Virginia Co (the VSCA), sets forth the requirements for a corporation under Virginia law.

The Delaware General Corporation Law, Title 8, Chapter 1 of the Delaware Code (the DGCL), sets forth the requirements for a corporation under Delaware law.

Key practice point: All directors and officers of a Virginia corporation should be familiar with the VSCA, and all directors and officers of a Delaware corporation should be familiar with the DGCL.

LLCs

The Virginia Limited Liability Company Act, Title 13.1, Chapter 12 of the Virginia Code (the VA LLC Act), sets forth the requirements for an LLC under Virginia law.

The Delaware Limited Liability Company Act, Title 8, Chapter 18 of the Delaware Code (the DE LLC Act) sets forth the requirements for an LLC under Delaware law.

Key practice point: All members, managers, and officers of a Virginia LLC should be familiar with the VA LLC Act, and all members, managers, and officers of a Delaware LLC should be familiar with the DE LLC Act.

3. Basic structural considerations

Corporations

The owners of a corporation are referred to as "shareholders" under Virginia law and "stockholders" under Delaware law.

- The owners of a corporation elect and remove individuals who serve on the corporation's board of directors, approve fundamental corporate actions (amendments to formation documents) and fundamental corporate transactions (mergers, sales of all or substantially all of the entity's assets).
- Shareholders (stockholders) can take action at a duly called meeting or by written action in lieu of a meeting, unless the formation documents preclude action without a meeting.

Under both the VSCA and the DGCL, all power and authority of a corporation is exercised by or under the direction of the corporation's board of directors, except as otherwise expressly provided in the incorporation document or the applicable statute.

- The number of members constituting the board of directors of a corporation may be set forth in the formation document, the bylaws, or by resolution of the board itself.
- A corporation's board of directors elects and removes officers—principally a president, secretary, and treasurer—and delegates to them the responsibilities of running the corporation's day-to-day operations.

- Under the applicable state law, there are certain actions that a corporation cannot take lawfully without board of director action, including amending the formation document after shares of capital stock have been issued; issuing shares of capital stock; declaring and paying dividends; and engaging in material transactions, such as mergers, acquisitions, and divestitures.
- The board of directors is also responsible for adopting "bylaws," the basic internal rules for the corporation's operations, and "corporate policies" covering topics such as: document retention and destruction; conflicts of interest; insider trading (if the corporation is public); and reporting and investigating allegations of improper activity ("whistleblowing").
- A board of directors can take action at a duly called meeting or by written action in lieu of a meeting (unless the formation documents preclude action without a meeting).

LLCs

The owners of an LLC are referred to as "members" under both Virginia law and Delaware law.

Both the VA LLC Act and the DE LLC Act vest full responsibility for managing the business and affairs of an LLC with the members, unless otherwise expressly provided in the entity's formation documents.

The members of an LLC may, in the formation documents, delegate the responsibility for managing the business and affairs of the entity to one or more "managers" (who may be authorized to act individually or as a board).

Some LLCs are structured to operate in substantially the same way as a corporation, and have formation documents that incorporate the various rules and regulations applicable to a corporation.

4.   Formation

Corporations

Virginia

A corporation is formed under Virginia law by filing articles of incorporation with the Virginia State Corporation Commission. These records are readily available to the public and, therefore, not confidential.

The VSCA requires the articles of incorporation to include the name of the entity, the number of shares of capital stock the entity is authorized to issue, a description of any classes or series of the capital stock, and information about the corporation's initial registered office and its initial registered agent.

The VSCA further provides that the articles of incorporation may include, among other things: information about the initial directors; provisions allowing for or precluding preemptive rights of shareholders to acquire unissued shares of capital stock; provisions regarding the management of the business and regulation of the corporation's affairs; and sections defining, limiting, and regulating the powers of the corporation, its directors, and shareholders.

Delaware

A corporation is formed under Delaware law by filing a certificate of incorporation with the Delaware Secretary of State. These records are readily available to the public and, therefore, not confidential.

The DGCL requires the certificate of incorporation to include the name of the entity, information about the corporation's registered office and its registered agent in Delaware, the nature of the business or purposes to be conducted, the number of shares of capital stock the entity is authorized to issue, a description of any classes or series of the capital stock, information about the incorporator(s), and information about the initial directors if the powers of the incorporator(s) terminate on the filing.

The DGCL further provides that the certificate of incorporation may include, among other things: any provision for the management of the business and for the conduct of the affairs of the corporation, and any provision creating, defining, limiting, and regulating the powers of the corporation, the directors, and the stockholders, or any class of stockholders, if such provisions are not contrary to Delaware law; provisions allowing for preemptive rights of stockholders to acquire unissued shares of capital stock; and provisions regarding the management of the business and regulation of the corporation's affairs.

Key practice point: All directors and officers of a corporation should be familiar with the corporation's articles or certificate of incorporation and any amendments thereto.

LLCs

Virginia

An LLC is organized under Virginia law by filing articles of organization with the Virginia State Corporation Commission. These records are readily available to the public and, therefore, not confidential.

The VA LLC Act requires the articles of organization to include the name of the entity, information about the LLC's initial registered office and its initial registered agent in Virginia, and the address of the LLC's principal office, if any (which may be outside Virginia).

The VA LLC Act further provides that the articles of organization may include any other matter that is permitted to be included in an operating agreement for an LLC.

Delaware

An LLC is formed under Delaware law by filing a certificate of formation with the Delaware Secretary of State. These records are readily available to the public and, therefore, not confidential.

The DE LLC Act requires the certificate of formation to include the name of the entity, information about the LLC's registered office, and its registered agent in Delaware.

The DE LLC Act further provides that the certificate of formation may include any other matters that the members determine to include therein.

Key practice point: Most certificates of formation contain only the basic information required under the VA/DE LLC Act.

5. Internal rules and regulations.

Corporations—Bylaws

The basic internal rules for a corporation's operations are contained in its bylaws.

The bylaws cover such subjects as: the manner, place, and time for calling and holding meetings of shareholders (or stockholders) and directors; the number and powers of the directors; the formation of committees of the board of directors; the duties and obligations of corporate officers; the requirements for certificates evidencing ownership of the corporation and transfers thereof; and indemnification of directors and officers.

The bylaws are not filed with any regulatory authority and are, therefore, generally not available to the public (unless the corporation itself is public, in which case they will be filed with the U.S. Securities and Exchange Commission).

Key practice point: All directors and officers should be familiar with the corporation's bylaws and any amendments thereto.

LLCs—Operating agreement/LLC agreement

The basic internal rules for an LLC's operations may be contained in an agreement entered into by the members, generally referred to as an "operating agreement" under the VA LLC Act and a "limited liability company agreement" under the DE LLC Act.

The VA LLC Act and the DE LLC Act provide default rules for management of an LLC if the members do not adopt an operating/LLC agreement.

The operating/LLC agreement is not filed with any regulatory authority and is, therefore, generally not available to the public (unless the LLC itself is public, in which case the agreement will be filed with the U.S. Securities and Exchange Commission).

Key practice point: All members and managers, if any, of an LLC should be familiar with the entity's operating/LLC agreement, and any amendments thereto.

6.   Conclusion

All senior executives of a company should have a working understanding of the company's form (corporation or LLC) the basic governance issues associated with that type of business entity.

ဇာ   ဇာ   ဇာ

Chapter 2

Maintaining Corporate Records

*David J. Charles, Pillsbury Winthrop Shaw Pittman LLP, and Michele Cappello,
NCI Information Systems, Inc.*

A corporation must maintain complete and accurate records of all official actions. A corporation's official records serve as evidence that it is following all of the formal requirements prescribed by applicable state law and is, therefore, afforded all of the rights, privileges, and protections of a corporation under those laws. This chapter highlights the principles for maintaining good corporate records for Virginia and Delaware corporations.

Corporate record book

Charter documents
The first document in a well-organized corporate record book (sometimes referred to as a "minute book) will be the formation document (either articles of incorporation for a Virginia corporation or a certificate of incorporation for a Delaware corporation, but referred to herein as the "charter").

Any amendments to the charter should be maintained as the second set of items in the corporation's official record book.

Generally, the bylaws will appear as the next item in a well-organized minute book. Any amendments to the bylaws should be filed with the bylaws. Bylaw amendments nullify any conflicting provisions in the initial bylaws or any previous amendments thereto, so keeping them in proper chronological order is critical.

The charter, as amended, together with the bylaws, as amended, are sometimes referred to as the "charter documents."

Official actions

Shareholders/stockholders

After the bylaws, the minute book should contain written evidence of all official actions taken by the shareholders (or stockholders).

Under both Virginia law and Delaware law, the owners of a corporation can take action either at a duly called meeting or by written action.

The minute book should include the official notice of any meeting of the shareholders (or stockholders) and a written record (or "minutes") summarizing the proceedings. An individual, often the corporation's secretary, is designated as the secretary of the meeting and charged with the task of preparing minutes for that meeting. Before filing the minutes with the corporate records, the secretary should sign and date the minutes to verify their authenticity.

If the shareholders (or stockholders) take action without a meeting by written action, that document, as executed by the requisite number of shareholders (or stockholders) to be effective, should also be filed in the corporate record book together with the notices and minutes of actual meetings.

Board of directors

Next, the minute book should contain written evidence of all official actions taken by the board of directors.

Under both Virginia law and Delaware law, the board of directors of a corporation can take action either at a duly called meeting or by written action.

The minute book should include the official notice of any meeting of the board of directors and minutes summarizing the proceedings. An individual (often the corporation's secretary) is designated as the secretary of the meeting and charged with the task of preparing minutes for that meeting. Before filing the minutes of a board of directors meeting with the corporate records, the secretary should circulate the minutes to each member of the board of directors for review, comment and approval. Once the minutes of a board of directors meeting are approved by the directors, the secretary should sign and date them to verify their authenticity.

If the board of directors takes action without a meeting by written action, that document, as executed by all of the members of the board of directors, should also be filed in the corporate record book together with the notices and minutes of actual meetings.

Key practice points: (1) Minutes of meetings by the board of directors or shareholders/ stockholders should summarize the discussions and actions and not attempt to record the proceedings verbatim.

(2) Written evidence of actions by the board of directors or shareholders/stockholders should be kept in chronological or reverse chronological order.

Stock ledger
A corporation that does not use a third-party transfer agent for transactions involving its capital stock must keep a written record of all issuances, transfers, redemptions, and cancellations of its capital stock. This record is typically referred to as the "stock ledger."

The stock ledger must contain a current list of all holders of issued and outstanding shares of capital stock, and should include up-to-date contact information for each such holder (addresses, phone numbers, fax numbers and, if available, email addresses). The entries on the stock ledger should indicate how many shares (by class and/or series, as applicable) each holder owns of record, and also include the dates the shares of capital stock were issued and the price paid for the shares.

The stock ledger is sometimes maintained apart from the minute book.

Stock certificates
If the corporation has certificated shares, a specimen certificate, as approved by the board of directors, should be maintained in the official records.

Corporations that issue certificates to evidence shares of capital stock should maintain copies of all such certificates. These are often included with the stock ledger in the official record books.

Blank stock certificates should be kept in a secure place, such as a safe or safety deposit box.

When shares of a corporation's capital stock are resold, new certificates should be issued to the new shareholders/stockholders for the number of shares acquired, and the old certificates should be marked "cancelled" and inserted in the corporation's record book. The transfer information should be completed on both the old and new stock certificate receipts, which should be maintained in the stock ledger, and the stock ledger should be updated to reflect the transaction.

Regulatory filings

Foreign qualification
If a corporation transacts business in a jurisdiction other than its jurisdiction of formation, it may have to qualify to do business in that jurisdiction as a "foreign corporation," depending on the level of activity it conducts in that jurisdiction. This is accomplished by filing a special application. Once the application has been processed and accepted, the state will issue an official certificate evidencing the entity's qualification to conduct business in that jurisdiction. This document should be maintained with the corporate records. If transacting business in a foreign jurisdiction, a registered agent is required to accept service of any legal or regulatory documents.

Annual reports
A corporation has to file periodic reports and pay applicable franchise taxes to remain in "good standing" in its jurisdiction of formation and each other jurisdiction where it is qualified to do business as a foreign corporation. Copies of these reports, and "good standing" certificates issued by the jurisdictions, should be maintained in the minute book with other regulatory filings.

Securities filings

A corporation should maintain copies of any filings it makes with the U.S. Securities and Exchange Commission (SEC) and any state securities regulatory agencies with its official corporate records.

Tax filings
A corporation should maintain copies of its EIN/TIN application (Form SS-4) and, if applicable, election to be treated as an S corporation (Form 1362), including any official correspondence from the Internal Revenue Service (IRS) with respect thereto, in its minute book.

Conclusion

A company must maintain complete and accurate records of all official actions in order to ensure that it will receive all of the rights, privileges, and protections available to it under applicable law.

Notes

Chapter 3

Corporate Compliance Programs

David J. Charles, Pillsbury Winthrop Shaw Pittman LLP, and Michele Cappello,
NCI Information Systems, Inc.

A corporate compliance program sets forth a code of conduct that defines proper business ethics within an organization. The process of creating the program requires a company to assess risk areas within its organization, minimizing the likelihood of any misconduct that could result in civil or criminal liability.

A corporation can face liability as an entity for the acts or omissions (failures to act) of its employees and agents as individuals. Corporations are "legal persons," capable of committing crimes, being sued, and being convicted. If an officer, director, employee, or agent of a corporation violates the law in an effort to further the company's business, or to further his or her own standing within the company, then the company can face criminal and civil penalties. The Federal Sentencing Guidelines provide for reduced sanctions and penalties if the defendant corporation has a real and effective corporate compliance program.

Effective compliance and ethics program

The Federal Sentencing Guidelines provide general and specific standards a corporation must follow in order to establish a real and effective corporate compliance program and, therefore, be eligible for reduced sanctions and penalties. As a threshold matter, the organization must exercise due diligence to prevent and detect criminal conduct, and otherwise promote an organizational culture that encourages ethical conduct and a commitment to compliance with the law. Specifically, this means:

- The corporation must have clear rules. These can take the form of separate policy statements regarding appropriate conduct, or they can be bundled into a single code of conduct or ethics manual. The code or manual should lay out the standards of conduct expected of all directors, officers, employees, and agents; the procedures for how individuals may report apparent violations of the rules; and how the company will respond to such reports, in each case as clearly as possible.

- The corporation must task "high-level" individuals—usually, executive officers—with the responsibility for ensuring that the company's business practices comply with the company's code of conduct, that the company's compliance training programs are effective, and that prompt and effective remedial action is taken when there is a violation of the code of conduct. In effect, the corporation must create a chain of command for implementing and maintaining its corporate compliance program that runs from the bottom to the top of the organization. Generally, corporations will appoint "ethics managers" who are close to each business unit and report directly to a "chief ethics officer" (or chief compliance officer), frequently the general counsel or chief financial officer, who in turn reports to the audit committee of the board of directors, or the board of directors itself. Further, the corporation must give such individuals adequate resources, appropriate authority, and direct access to the highest levels of authority within the organization.

- The corporation must exercise due care to avoid delegating substantial discretionary authority to individuals whom the organization knows, or should know through the exercise of due diligence, are likely to engage in illegal activities. Companies satisfy this requirement by conducting background checks on new hires who are expected to have substantial discretionary authority, as well as existing employees who are being given increased responsibility.

- The corporation must take reasonable steps to communicate periodically and in a practical manner the code of conduct by conducting an effective training program.

- The corporation must take reasonable steps to achieve compliance with its standards. This requirement encompasses a number of aspects. Companies have to conduct period reviews at all levels to assess whether their employees are complying with the code of conduct. In addition, companies have to establish systems or procedures that enable employees to report instances of misconduct without the fear of retribution. Many companies install a hotline for these purposes. The corporation must also evaluate the efficacy of its compliance program periodically.

- The standards of conduct must be consistently applied and enforced.
- The corporation must take remedial action promptly. The remedial action is not limited to disciplining the employee, agent, or officer who breached the company's code of conduct. As part of the remedial action, a corporation must also assess its compliance program, how it functioned in the particular case, and how it can be improved.

Key practice point: When considering a corporate compliance program, it is important to remember the three Cs: clear rules; compliance with those rules; and consistent enforcement and maintenance of those rules.

Scope of code of conduct

Every corporation should assess its operations to determine those areas that pose the greatest risk of legal exposure, and/or where compliance procedures are otherwise perceived to be necessary. The following list reflects some of the areas that are frequently covered by compliance programs:

- Conflicts of interest
- Misuse of company funds or assets
- Reporting and investigating allegations of improper activity (whistleblowing)
- Company books and records
  - ◇ Proper maintenance
  - ◇ Retention/destruction policies
- Labor/employment
  - ◇ Factory conditions
  - ◇ Discrimination
  - ◇ Harassment
- Improper payments/benefits/bribery
- Foreign Corrupt Practices Act (FCPA)
- Insider trading (if the corporation is public)
- Export controls
- Gifts and gratuities (to customers, suppliers, subcontractors)
- Lobbying and political activity
- Drug-free workplace

Regular certification

Every corporation should require all of its employees to certify that they have read the code of conduct when they are hired and annually thereafter, along with annual training based on the code of conduct. The corporation should keep an accurate record of all such certifications and training participation.

Federal government contractors

Subpart 3.10 of the Federal Acquisition Regulation, implemented in December 2007, specifically requires certain federal government contractors to have a written code of business ethics and conduct and an effective compliance program.

Conclusion

A company can reduce potential exposure for civil and criminal liability by adopting and implementing an effective compliance program that defines proper business ethics within the organization.

Edwards Brothers,Inc!
Thorofare, NJ 08086
13 April, 2011
BA2011103